The

Art of Kissing

BOOK OF QUESTIONS
AND ANSWERS

Praise for *The Art of Kissing* by **William Cane**

❧ "Whoever said 'a kiss is just a kiss' didn't get his mitts on *The Art of Kissing. . . .* A detailed how-to book . . . this year's handy alternative to chocolates."

—*Elle*

❧ "Some terrific tips on how you can make every kiss as passionate and thrilling as your first."

—*The National Enquirer*

❧ "I advise you to race full speed to your bookstore and pick up a copy of *The Art of Kissing* . . . it could save you emotional problems."

—*Clarion Ledger* (Jackson, Mississippi)

❧ "If you want to smooch like Rick and Elsa in *Casablanca,* this bussing bible is for you."

—Lowell (Massachusetts) *Sun*

❧ "The definitive book . . . lighthearted . . . fun . . . worth more than lip service!"

—Oxford (England) *Mail*

Also by William Cane

The Art of Kissing

The Book of Kisses

The Art of Hugging

The

Art of Kissing

BOOK OF QUESTIONS
AND ANSWERS

William Cane

St. Martin's Griffin
New York

Production Editor: David Stanford Burr

Library of Congress Cataloging-in-Publication Data

Cane, William.
    The art of kissing book of questions and answers / William Cane.—1st St. Martin's Griffin ed.
        p.   cm.
    Includes index.
    ISBN 0-312-19830-2
    1. Kissing.   2. Questions and answers.   I. Title.
GT2640.C363   1999
394—dc21   98-46413
                                                                                   CIP

First St. Martin's Griffin Edition: February 1999

10   9   8   7   6   5   4   3   2   1

For my friend Christy Garza

Contents

$\mathcal{P}$REFACE

Congratulations! You're reading a book that may forever change the way you kiss. By the time you finish it, you'll have as much knowledge as a person who has kissed more than ten thousand people—the current data base from which these questions and answers were derived. (But your lips will be in much better shape!)

Why another book on kissing, you ask? After all, didn't my first book, *The Art of Kissing,* cover everything?

Sure, it covered everything—at the time. But there are always surprising developments in the world of kissing. This new book contains questions that readers around the world have asked me together with answers providing up-to-date information about kissing trends, tongue piercing, kissing someone new for the first time, kissing anxiety, and the best way to french kiss. There are also plenty of trendy new kisses including the elevator kiss, the Valentine's Day kiss, the comet kiss, the anniversary kiss, the grudge kiss, the emotionless kiss, the *new* hand kiss, the slip-off kiss, the frog kiss, and much more! How a person could go through life without knowing about these kisses is beyond me. When you buy this book you're not just buying words on paper—you're really buying the collective experience of ten thousand kissing lovers. And when you go on a date, they'll all be in your corner, rooting for you to try their kissing tricks and techniques. There's so much new information here that I can't summarize it all in the preface. Which is a terrific reason to keep this book on your coffee table when your dates visit. Its very presence tends to validate kissing-only relationships that can be prolonged for weeks or even months . . . giving you time to find out whether it's safe to take that relationship to the next level.

You may never have attended one of my multimedia presentations in which college students demonstrate all these kisses onstage. But you'll benefit from the questions they asked during rehearsal. *Rehearsal?* Yes, of course—they have to practice the trendy ones like lip-o-suction and the vacuum kiss, unusual ones like upside-down and sliding kisses, and bizarre ones like biting and Trobriand Islands kisses. They learn and perform more than twenty-five different types of kisses in all. Before you know it you'll be prepared to kiss upside down in a foreign country while driving—and that's just for starters. Among other things, you'll also learn why you shouldn't ask for a kiss, what to do if someone drools on you, and how to convince your boyfriend or girlfriend to change their kissing style.

Specific sections also clue you in on what the opposite sex likes best. Girls will discover what kinds of kisses boys are dying to get. They'll also learn how to encourage boys to kiss romantically, like guys in movies do. Guys will learn why they should kiss their girlfriend's neck and ears more often. They'll also discover that women view kissing with vastly different expectations from their own.

But before we get to the good stuff, I'd like to thank all who helped with the data collection, especially the hundreds of students who participated in kissing demonstrations across the country and the more than ten thousand people, ages nine to sixty-two, who asked questions of mike@kissing.com or visited the art of kissing web page at www.kissing.com to help fine-tune the answers. Thanks also to two talented and good-natured lecture agents, Jayne and Kevin Moore at the Contemporary Issues Agency. I'm also indebted to Mitch Douglas at ICM for his wise counsel and advocacy and to Marian Lizzi for making the book more romantic. Last but not least I must thank the dentists who took a break from—*Whrrrrrrrrrrrrrr* goes the drill! . . . "Who's on the phone? . . . The kissing guy? . . . Lean forward and spit! I'll finish drilling in a minute"—to answer my technical questions about oral pleasure.

Now let's have some fun—

M. C.
July 15, 1998

The
Art of Kissing
BOOK OF QUESTIONS
AND ANSWERS

CHAPTER ONE

Becoming a Better Kisser

Can I become a better kisser?

Yes, and here's why I'm convinced of it. One day this guy from Ohio calls me with a kissing question. "I'm afraid to let my girl-friend see that I have your book *The Art of Kissing* because I don't want her to think I'm practicing."

"Are you crazy? She'll love you for having it. She'll think it's romantic. Read the book, practice the kisses, then call me back."

I thought that was the end of it.

Two weeks later he calls back!

"I took your advice and read the book. I mentally practiced some of the kisses, and when my girlfriend came over, I started doing them to her. I was nervous at first, worried she'd think it was weird. But she didn't complain at all. In fact, while I was kissing her she started moaning. Then she said she felt like she was melting. And I screamed in my mind to you, 'Thank you, thank you, thank you!' "

Can you become a better kisser? Of course you can. Just like that fellow from Ohio. You can learn some new techniques and try them with your lover. The entire purpose of this book is to teach you something new so that by the end of the evening your partner will be moaning and saying they feel like they're melting. And you'll be getting all the credit when it was actually ten thousand other people who did the fieldwork. How's that for a deal?

Are some people better kissers than others?

More than 80 percent of men and women say yes—some people are definitely better. The real question, of course, is what makes one kisser better than another? And how can you improve?

There are several things you can do to make yourself a better kisser. Some of the factors that women say make a man a better kisser include passion, sensitivity, creativity, and variety. Typical is this comment from a thirty-year-old who says, "I prefer kissing a guy who has a clean mouth/fresh minty breath, who gently rolls his tongue about mine, and has the same rhythm or sync as me. Also one who doesn't dribble. One who can be passionate yet gentle enough to convey his feelings for me through the kiss." Men generally consider women better kissers if they open their mouth more, try more french kisses, and don't demand too much when kissing—such as hugging and saying loving things. For both men and women, responsiveness is the chief factor that makes for a better kisser. This means being aware of your partner's likes and dislikes and changing your kissing style to suit them. So, the bottom line when it comes to being a better kisser is knowing more ways to kiss so that you can adapt to your lover. The rest of this book is aimed at helping you do just that.

Why do people kiss?

People kiss primarily because they're conditioned to by their culture. Which is good news for all of us. In the United States, as well as the rest of the Western Hemisphere and Europe, people actually feel an unconscious obligation to kiss when they find themselves in a romantic situation. This is one of the most useful discoveries I made in my research. Members of the opposite sex are out there just waiting to kiss. It's almost like they've been programmed to do it. And once you realize this, you can get a lot more kisses and enjoy kissing more.

This conditioning or cultural programming occurs on a daily basis. People see actors kissing on television, in movies, and in advertisements. They hear stories about friends and lovers kissing. They see people kissing in public. As a result, they expect that kissing will occur in certain situations. When they find themselves in a romantic situation, those unconscious forces will be brought into play—they'll feel an almost irresistible impulse to kiss, whether they consciously want to or not!

Is there any other reason why people kiss?

Kissing also satisfies a universal biological drive for oral stimulation. This powerful drive is one of the reasons that you enjoy eating and drinking. Kissing is second only to eating and drinking in satisfying this primal urge for oral stimulation. If you want evidence of this oral urge, look at people chewing gum, smoking cigarettes, biting their nails, gnawing on pencil erasers. Observe people eating in restaurants, licking ice-cream cones, sipping drinks in bars. Everywhere you go, people are satisfying their oral desires. Some even satisfy oral needs by talking. And that's the kind of cumulative oral energy that lies behind every kiss. When your lover kisses you, they're putting all their other oral activities on hold and expressing their oral desires through lip contact. Once you realize this, you can become more sensitive to your partner's oral needs when kissing. And by satisfying those needs, you will be perceived as a better kisser. For example, right after one woman met her husband, she learned that he loved gum. "I used to let him chew on my tongue, and it satisfied him. Seven years later, he still loves kissing me. You should see my tongue, though."

Are there any emotional reasons for kissing?

Yes, in addition to satisfying an oral desire, kissing also brings people close, physically and emotionally. There was a joke on *Seinfeld* in which one character asked, "Why does sex make for intimacy? Is it something in the fluids exchanged?" The humor in this silly question is that it ignores the real answer, which is simple. Sex brings people close physically, which results in more time being spent together. From this shared time together, intimacy develops. Fluids have nothing to do with it! You can't kiss without being close. As a result, most people spend time getting close to their partner before a kiss, and they stay close afterward, too. This closeness satisfies a deep emotional need for connection with others.

How can I make myself more kissable?

The Swedes have a great word, *kysstäck,* which means kissable. For them the entire concept of being kissable is serious business. In the West, we don't use the word "kissable" all that much. You primarily hear it in toothpaste and breath-mint commercials.

And the first way to make yourself more kissable is to work on your breath. Brush your teeth. Floss. Use mouthwash, although its effect lasts only about an hour. And most important, brush your tongue, which will remove bacteria and freshen it, leaving your breath sweet and clean.

But there are more ways to make yourself kissable than by simply working on your breath. Few people realize it, but being funny can increase your kissability score with the opposite sex. Both men and women like someone with a good sense of humor. Learn a few jokes and drop them into conversations.

For women, you can also increase your kissability index by dressing in an attractive way, wearing your hair in a stylish cut, and smiling more. Lipstick isn't that important. Most men (67 percent) don't mind if you wear it, 25 percent dislike it, and 8 percent like it if it is flavored. You may want to keep that in mind when selecting your next brand.

Men can increase their kissability index by being taller (try wearing boots or shoes with heels) and by acting friendly. In a recent survey, more women were attracted to Woody Allen than Arnold Schwarzenegger, suggesting that humor is more important than brawn and good looks. Most women (53 percent) prefer a clean-shaven guy, but a surprisingly large percent (33 percent) occasionally like kissing a guy who has stubble. Says one young woman, "When he kisses me without shaving, he looks like a cowboy and I just want to ride away with him." You might want to try showing up for a date sometime without shaving. She just might like it.

How can I get my boyfriend to kiss me?

The way to get a guy to kiss you is to take the initiative. Flirt. But you may have to make the first move. Don't hesitate to do it. He'll be flattered, though possibly surprised. Make sure your breath is fresh by chewing gum or mints beforehand. Wait for the right moment, when you're feeling romantic, maybe after a date or in a romantic spot. Stand close to him. If necessary, take tiny little steps toward him to crowd him back against a wall so he can't get away. Perfume. A flirtatious touch. How could he resist?

If all else fails, tell him he has nice shoulders—this will flatter him. Lots of young guys do push-ups and are proud of their deltoid muscles, but girls almost never notice this. As you tell him, move in close. Put your hands up to his shoulders and feel his muscles. Then continue standing close. Look up into his eyes. If he still hasn't made a move, tell him he has nice hair, nice ears, a nice voice—anything. Keep complimenting him. If he's into sports, tell him you'd love to see him in his uniform. Then take a few more tiny little steps toward him so that he can smell your perfume. If he still hasn't done anything, push your chest into his and say, "I bet you'd be good at football."

You may find yourself fighting him off.

What if I'm afraid of being rejected?

Believe it or not, a stunningly attractive young woman at a Missouri college told me she was afraid of being rejected by her guy friend, who she wanted to kiss.

"Why would anyone reject you? You're absolutely gorgeous."

"Thank you. But, this guy and I have been wrestling when we get together and—"

"Wrestling?"

"Yes."

"Physically wrestling?"

"Yes. You know, like play wrestling."

"And he doesn't kiss you?"

"No! He never has."

"I find that hard to believe."

"I swear it's true."

"Why doesn't he?"

"I think he just wants to keep it on a friendly basis. But I want to kiss him. I'm just afraid of being rejected."

The answer here is that at a certain point you have to take a chance. I told her that there was no way in the world any guy would reject her physically, but not all guys would be compatible with her emotionally. She was kind of an independent woman, and a bit assertive. And not all guys like that. So she might get the guy to kiss her, but then be disappointed later on if he didn't fall in love with her.

The best way to deal with your emotional insecurity is to wait for plenty of eye contact before you kiss your partner. Eye contact is a sign of interest. And prolonged eye contact usually occurs during a good conversation. These particular two people had gone way beyond eye contact, however. They had progressed to the point where they were regularly rolling around on the couch, wrestling! At this point, you can safely assume that the other person is at least physically attracted to you. In such a situation, it's safe to risk a kiss.

One footnote for beautiful women and extremely handsome guys: Research suggests that members of the opposite sex are often shy around good-looking people. Many beautiful women say that guys won't call them and ask for a date because they're afraid of being rejected. As a result, they often have fewer dates than average-looking people. And they often can't tell if someone really likes them for themselves or just for their looks. Ironically, in such a situation, many good-looking women have resorted to becoming more aggressive about initiating contact with the guys they like, which results in more dates and more kissing opportunities.

Can I tell if a guy likes me by the way he kisses?

Sometimes, but not always. Many women believe that tender, gentle, almost feathery kisses signal a guy's romantic interest. On the other hand, guys who are just interested in sex, it is often believed, are more apt to rush on to using their tongue in a kiss. That line from "The Shoop Shoop Song"—"If you want to know if he loves you so, it's in his kiss"—has undoubtedly contributed to this reliance on kissing as an indicator of a man's true feelings.

In reality, things are a little more complicated. First of all, you're not thinking clearly when you're kissing, so your judgment is liable to be biased. And while the song lyrics may sound terrific, they're also somewhat misleading. Sure, a gentle kiss may indicate true romantic interest, and a tongue kiss may signal nothing more than sexual desire. But guys who have predatory interests can also kiss gently, especially at the outset. They aren't idiots—they know what you like, and they can kiss as romantically as the best of them. Which isn't to say that you should become cynical. Just keep your wits about you and don't get lulled into an overreliance on kissing style as an indicator of a guy's true romantic interest.

It's much more important, especially at the outset of a relationship, to observe how a guy talks and looks at you during a conversation. Admittedly, kissing style may indicate something about how he feels. But the way he talks and listens is usually a much more reliable way to measure his interest. A guy who keeps glancing at other women or whose attention isn't focused on you is probably not your best bet. But a guy who talks in a friendly way, maintains appropriate eye contact, laughs easily, and is able to carry on a good conversation by listening as well as talking is probably more romantically interested in you. So don't just rely on his kissing technique. Observe how he interacts with you in conversations and whether he shares your interests. Often that's an even better indicator of true compatibility.

How can I kiss my girlfriend to prove that I love her?

Since many women judge the sincerity of your intentions by the way you kiss, if you give her a french kiss right away, she's liable to write you off as someone who's only interested in sex. But if you kiss her gently and tenderly, you're more likely to convince her that you really enjoy being with her. When you give a woman soft, lingering lip kisses, she's apt to think, "Ooooo! This one really cares!"

Why does kissing on the lips for guys not mean the same as it does for girls?

The twenty-one-year-old woman who asked this went on to say, "What I mean is that when a guy kisses me on the lips, it means something special to me—that he's very interested. But many of my guy friends say kissing doesn't mean a lot to them emotionally." The answer is that most boys are emotional infants compared to girls their age. They know all the right things to say and all the right moves to make to get a girl interested. They know the trick about gentle kisses on the lips. They're fully aware that girls will interpret it as a sign of interest. So they do it, and hope for the best. This is not to say that guys are users and manipulators of their girlfriends' feelings. Only that they may not be as deeply affected by the intimacy of a kiss as their girlfriends are. Naturally there are exceptions, and it may be worth your while to find them. For example, I recently heard from a guy who drove more than a thousand miles from New Jersey to Mississippi to give a girl he liked a hug. That kind of romantic interest is worth looking for.

Are there any differences between how men and women like to kiss?

There are many gender-based differences in kissing preferences, and throughout this book we'll examine them in great detail. In general, men are less sensitive to being kissed on different parts of their face and body. Women like neck and ear kisses much more than men. And most men like french kisses earlier in a relationship than women. By knowing what the opposite sex likes, you can increase your ability to please them when kissing.

How do I get a guy to kiss me softly and without there having to be tongues involved?

Most guys have to be told to kiss like this or they won't do it. One of the best ways to tell him is actually to show him. Begin by telling him you want to play a game. This game has one very simple rule—he's not allowed to kiss you back for one full minute. During that minute, you're going to kiss him the way you like to be kissed. Then give him those gentle lip kisses. He should be able to learn from your example. Teach him by kissing him gently.

Lots of women have asked this question. In addition to the game, there are two other ways to get a guy to kiss you gently. One is easy, the other is rather dangerous.

The easy way is to wait for a time when you're not kissing. Use that opportunity to bring up the subject of kissing. Maybe you can do it when you see a couple kissing in public or on television or in the movies. Tell your boyfriend how you like to be kissed. If he listens to you, he may learn how to do it the way you like.

The second way, which is more dangerous, was developed by the renowned psychologist B. F. Skinner. It's called conditioning your boyfriend. This technique works on dogs and pigeons, so it should also work on your boyfriend because, after all, he's an animal, isn't he? You begin by telling him that you want gentle kisses. You also insist that during this particular date you're going to try an experiment. Neither of you is going to be allowed to progress any further than simple hugs, caresses, and lip kisses. No french kissing allowed. Then you tell him that as a reward for behaving as and doing what you request, you'll wear his favorite sexy outfit.

And here's why it's dangerous . . . under these circumstances he's liable to want more than kisses. Which is why you have to really draw the line—kisses only, please! If you can get him to behave under these conditions, you'll both get something you dearly want. He'll get a visual show that should be enough to motivate any guy to do as you say. And you'll receive gentle, loving, tender kisses.

Is it wrong to teach my boyfriend to kiss the way I like?

No, it's the right thing to do! Most men are delighted to find out what their girlfriends like. Lots of guys complain that they don't know what their dates enjoy. You'll be doing yourself and him a big favor by letting him know your kissing preferences.

How can a guy tell if he's a good kisser?

You know you're a good kisser if both you and your partner like how it feels. Observe her reactions when you kiss her. If she looks bored, chances are you're not lighting her fire. If she giggles, blushes, sweats, squirms around, and emits little squeaks of pleasure . . . need I say more? You've got to learn to read a woman like a book, or at least like the sports pages. It's not too hard, really. It's kind of simple common sense.

Sometimes after kissing she'll say, "You're a good kisser." But sometimes she'll just moan and look dreamy. Women may fake other things, but they almost never fake their reactions when kissing.

How can a girl tell if she's a good kisser?

The top ten ways to tell if you're a good kisser are—

10. He lets you kiss him during football games.
9. He comes right out and says, "You kiss better than my last girlfriend."
8. He shakes, sweats, or laughs uncontrollably when you kiss him.

7. He mentions your kissing skills to friends and swears them to secrecy, but it gets back to you anyway.
6. He gasps for breath between kisses but quickly comes back for more.
5. He kisses you for the sake of kissing, without trying to pressure you into heavy petting.
4. He doesn't offer you a breath mint when you kiss him.
3. He never talks about your kissing skills with male friends. (He's keeping a good thing to himself.)
2. He sometimes cries when he kisses you but claims it was just dust that got in his eye.
1. He closes his eyes, hugs you, and smiles like a baby when you kiss him.

What are the signs that I'm a bad kisser?

The top ten signs that you need to improve your kissing skills are—

10. When you approach for a kiss, your girlfriend looks terrified, as if she's on a killer roller coaster.
9. Your partner gags while kissing.
8. Your partner is covered in saliva after a kiss.
7. Your partner never giggles, moans, or shakes uncontrollably when you kiss.
6. Your partner looks like he or she is reading the *Wall Street Journal* during a kiss.
5. Your partner stops kissing you back so that you're left doing all the work.
4. After a kiss, your partner asks, in an excited voice, if you've seen the evening news.

3. Your partner looks distracted.

2. Your partner falls asleep.

1. Your partner says something rude, like, "What other tricks do you know?"

What is the biggest mistake I can make when kissing?

The worst thing you can do is forget about your partner's feelings and reactions. Kissing is an oral pleasure, so sometimes you're perfectly justified in focusing on your own enjoyment. It's quite similar to the enjoyment you'd get from eating your favorite food. (Just think how delicious it feels to eat french fries or a baked potato with butter and salt.) But some people are so entranced with their own pleasure, they forget about their partner's reactions. Remember, your partner is more than a baked potato—he or she has feelings, emotions, and expectations, and it's a mistake to ignore them.

How can I become a better kisser?

The easiest way to become a better kisser is to practice. The same way you can practice your golf swing or your piano lessons, you can practice kissing. The reason that practice helps you become a better kisser is that you learn what works and what doesn't, and you drill this into your memory.

Do I need a partner to practice?

No. You can practice and become a better kisser without a partner. You could do this in any number of fun ways. You could kiss your pillow. (Some people do.) You could kiss a picture in a magazine. (Some people do.) Or you could kiss your pet. (Some people do, despite how crazy it sounds.)

What is the best way to practice?

Use your imagination. Many studies have demonstrated that mental rehearsal is one of the most effective ways to improve your game. In fact, one study was conducted with college students, thirty of whom were selected and asked to throw a basketball into a hoop a hundred times. Their hits and misses were counted. Most only got it in about 15 percent of the time. Then one group was told to practice by throwing the ball for five minutes a day for a week. The second group was told not to practice. And the third group was instructed to practice mentally—just by sitting in a quiet place and thinking about throwing the ball successfully into the hoop. After the week was up, all three groups were tested again. The first group, which actually practiced, improved only slightly. The second group, which had no practice, actually did worse. And the third group, which practiced mentally, improved by more than 35 percent.

Professional sports psychologists and coaches have used studies like these to devise ways to train athletes. The same techniques can be used to become a better kisser.

Begin by imagining someone you'd like to kiss. Then sit back in an easy chair, close your eyes, and imagine kissing those lips, that mouth, that delicious face! Go over it in your mind until you can feel it. The more senses you bring into play, the better your mental rehearsal will work. Try to imagine what they smell like, what they sound like when they moan, what the temperature and pressure of their lips will feel like against yours.

How does mental rehearsal work?

According to Maxwell Maltz, author of the extraordinary self-help motivational book *Psycho-Cybernetics,* everyone has a subconscious mind that responds best to images and feelings. But the strangest thing is that the subconscious mind cannot tell the difference between fantasy and reality. So if you imagine kissing Miss America or Mr. Universe in enough detail, your subconscious mind will actually believe you did it. Then when you kiss your boyfriend or girlfriend, your previous mental rehearsal will give you a boost of confidence. Since you've already kissed Miss America or Mr. Universe, kissing your boyfriend or girlfriend will be a breeze.

How can I get my guy to kiss me like they do in those romantic movies?

I actually included this question less for the gals than for the *guys* reading the book. Take note, guys, what kinds of questions gals are asking over and over. They want you to be romantic. They want experiences like in the movies. They want romance, adventure, togetherness, tenderness. And if you know this, you can deliver the goods!

Be romantic for her. Walk with her along a river or down a side street. Tell her you like her company. Say something nice even if it kills you. And mean it. Then slow down. She'll slow down, too. She's hanging on your every word. Turn to her . . .

And kiss her!

Kiss her like there's no tomorrow.

Kiss her like she's going away forever and you'll never see her again. Kiss her like you mean it. Press yourself to her like you want to protect her from spies, enemies, and secret agents. Hold her in your arms and make her know you care. Whisper something in her ear. If you can't think of anything, tell her you love her if that's how you feel.

But kiss her!

Don't forget to kiss her with all your heart and soul.

And she'll never forget you did.

What's more important, technique or passion?

Passion. But technique isn't far behind in importance. For you to enjoy kissing any particular partner, they have to be a good kisser *and* you have to like them. If you like someone but they're a terrible kisser, it won't be as much fun. Similarly, if you *don't* like someone, it won't matter if he looks like Leonardo DiCaprio, you probably won't enjoy it as much because the emotional connection is missing. You need both a good kisser plus an emotional connection for the best experience. And you deserve both. So keep looking for both, and you're bound to find them.

Which is ultimately more important, though, finding a good kisser or liking the person I'm kissing?

Of the two, there's no question that liking the person is by far the more important element. If you like someone, care for them, and love them, you'll almost always love kissing them, unless they drool excessively, in which case, see my advice on page 137–38. Plus you can usually teach someone—in subtle ways—to kiss a little better.

Can kissing tell me what someone is really like?

Sometimes kissing can tell you more about a person than listening in on their therapy sessions. When we kiss we regress. We go back to an earlier stage of our psychosexual development. In fact, we regress to the oral, infantile stage. And at that moment, we become a baby again. Which is why you often hear lovers cooing "I love you, baby" to each other at the height of their passion.

Observe your partner in this babyish state and you'll get a good idea what they're like deep down inside. One guy says he kissed a girl who used to suck his mouth like a baby bottle. "She was insatiable. She would suck like she was at her mother's breast and was afraid that breast was going to be yanked out of her mouth at any second. It horrified me! It actually terrified me sometimes. It really frightened me." This girl had deep emotional problems, which became very apparent during kissing. So observe your lover. You may find out things about them that will open your eyes and cause you sleepless nights. Or you may find that you love to regress right alongside them. Most important, the very fact that you're observing your partner so closely will help make you a better kisser.

CHAPTER TWO

First Kiss Jitters

What's the best way to kiss someone for the first time?

Start with someone you really like—someone who keeps you up nights thinking about him or her, someone who gets your blood hot and your nerves excited. When you're in the same room with this honey, your heart should race and you should feel slightly dizzy. If these are your reactions, this is the *right* person to start with—you've got all the classic symptoms of infatuation. Try giving him or her a good-night kiss at the end of a date, and do it when you're both sober, because you'll feel it more intensely and have your wits about you. You're going to need them because your first kiss with this dreamboat will do so many wonderful things to your physical and emotional makeup that you'll feel like you landed on another planet!

Why do you suggest trying a first kiss at the end of a date? And how do I actually do it?

This is one of the easiest times to accomplish a first kiss. During a date, you and your partner have a chance to talk at length. First-date conversations can be nerve-racking, but they can also be pleasantly exciting. You're sitting together in a coffee shop, looking at each other over a cup of steaming hot coffee, chatting about philosophy. But in the back of your mind you're thinking, I wonder what it would be like to kiss her? You look deeply into your partner's eyes. Why am I talking about philosophy, you think, when all I want to do is kiss? . . . And then you begin to hope that she's thinking the same thing.

You've never kissed, held hands, or hugged your date before. But while you're sitting together, your feet accidentally touch under the table. And at this accidental contact, a strong current of electricity runs through your body. It's like a powerful electric circuit has been closed, the shock so violent you can no longer concentrate on what your partner is saying. Your mind becomes numb. Your senses are paralyzed. Your mouth tingles with secret vibratory anticipation, as if your lips had been stung by a thousand invisible bees. Every nerve in your body seems to cry out, "Do something! Don't just sit there!"

Your palms begin to sweat. You can hear your heart beating in your chest. The sound is so loud, you wonder why no one is staring at you. *But someone is staring at you!* Your date is looking across the table right into your eyes. For a second, you think she can perhaps hear the pounding of your heart. What can it mean? Why is your date staring at you like this, with pupils dilated like two pools of black ink into which you feel you could fall at any moment and never emerge?

Somehow you manage to get to your feet. Your knees are weak. Now you're outside the shop, walking with your date. Side by side, you make your way up a hill. The stars burn brightly in the sky. Everything feels supremely romantic. But you keep regretting not having made a move in the coffee shop. You wonder if you've lost your chance. As you walk, one of your hands innocently brushes your date's, and again you feel an electric current zap through your body as if you've touched a high-voltage power line. Suddenly you're no longer walking. You find yourself standing stock-still, facing your date, moon-light flashing in her eyes. What's happening? You seem to be magnetized by an invisible force, drawing you toward your date like a sci-fi tractor beam.

What is this mad power she has over you? Why can't you break free? You can hardly breathe! Your heart pounds, your body trembles, your knees wobble like Jell-O. And you feel that there's absolutely nothing you can do at this moment—except kiss! For an instant, you wish you could turn and run as fast as your legs can carry you. But at this point, you know that's liter-ally impossible. Your legs are paralyzed! Strong electric shocks run over your limbs, through your nerves, and into your brain. If anyone took an X ray of you right now, you're sure that you and your partner would be outlined in a scintillating halo, a weird combination of fireworks, rainbow, and aurora borealis.

God help me! you're thinking. Has it come to this? Am I made for nothing more than a kiss? Suddenly the answer comes back, like the voice of your conscience booming inside your head, *Kiss her, you fool!* And then you're leaning forward. Your date's eyes seem to be swimming through the starry void toward you, her luminous face more beautiful than a Madonna and child by the greatest artist who ever painted, and you feel like you're floating in the summer breeze, lifting up off the hill, drifting ever closer toward your partner. And as you approach, you can actually smell the delicious perfume rising from her body. You feel like you're going to faint.

Her lips part, her even, white teeth flash in the darkness, and everything in your heart cries out for you to plant your mouth on hers. So what's holding you back? Why isn't the kiss happening? You seem to be encased in a straitjacket! It feels like your arms are imprisoned in a cocoon. Your limbs have all gone numb! You can hardly move. You feel so out of it! Maybe you're hallucinating! It feels like a dream! With a mighty effort you lean forward again. Everything seems to be happening in excruciating slow motion. And then, at last, you're so close that you can feel the heat from your date's lips on yours. Just the heat of her face and lips. How wonderful it feels! How inexplicably sinful and joyous! Like heaven on earth.

And then your lips touch! They actually touch! "Houston, the Eagle has landed!" Oh, dear God, what have you gotten yourself into this time! Lip contact! Lip contact!

Now what?

What do I do during a kiss?

Your partner's lips feel so good, so soft, so warm, so delicious! For a moment, you almost lose your mind and think it might be nice to take a bite out of them. Don't! Restrain your aggressive oral impulses. This is a first kiss, so take your time. Be nice, be gentle, be loving. Do what most people do during a first kiss— rock your head back and forth . . . ever so slowly.

Rock your head from side to side, gently, tentatively, as if you're asking your partner a question. Horses do this in the stall—they stand together and nuzzle their faces together. Your powers of mental reasoning have left you momentarily. You're conscious of nothing but the animal-like sensation of standing with your partner, nuzzling your faces together. You don't even have time to think about how good it feels. It just feels so natural, so easy, so perfect! Keep rocking your head back and forth, enjoying the sinfully soft sensation of your partner's lips on yours.

Should I open my mouth?

As you rock your head back and forth, keep your lips closed. This is closed-mouth dry kissing. Concentrate on your breathing. Breathe through your nose, inhaling the (hopefully!) delicious fragrance of your partner. And most important of all . . . relax! How, you ask? Make an effort to relax, especially your lips. Says one young woman, "I don't like guys who kiss with tight, tense lips. They've got to loosen up or they'll get no kisses from me!" One of the best ways to relax your lips during a first kiss is to keep this simple advice in mind: "If something is worth doing, it's worth doing poorly." That's right—poorly. In other words, don't try too hard. Too much effort sometimes makes things worse. Just get your lips in contact with your partner's and see what happens. If you concentrate a little more on the back of your head, your lips will relax automatically. Think about rocking your head back and forth during your first kiss, and let your lips take care of themselves.

Where does my nose go?

Here you are on a hilltop, having your first kiss, your lips in delicious contact, and you begin to rock your head, when suddenly—*thwannnnk!* Everything stops! Your noses have crashed! What do you do now? At this point some people throw up their hands in dismay and conclude that they weren't designed for

kissing. But this is a mistake. The human head was perfectly designed for kissing—if you know this one little secret. As soon as
your noses touch, tilt your head back just enough to run your
nose back up along your partner's nose until the tippy tips of
your noses are touching, all the while keeping your mouth
closed and your lips in contact with your partner's lips! As the
tips of your noses touch, tilt your head ever so slightly to the
side, allowing your noses to slip by one another like two ships
passing in the night.

Now you're on the other side, and you can continue rocking
your head back and forth indefinitely, your noses passing like this
every time.

How can I tell if a girl wants to be kissed?

Believe it or not, a lot of girls on dates are thinking, "When is
he ever going to kiss me?" That's because many guys are not
making the move soon enough for them. The best way to tell if
a girl wants you to kiss her is by the way she looks at you. If she
keeps looking away at other people and can't focus on you, then
she's not ready for a kiss. But if she looks steadily at you while
talking, if she allows you to gaze deeply into her eyes, then you
know the situation is moving in the right direction and she's getting comfortable with you, comfortable enough to allow you to
kiss her. There's no predefined number of seconds, so there's no
need to bring along a stopwatch. Use your own sense of the situation to determine when it seems like she's inviting you with
her eyes.

Can I tell if a girl wants to be kissed by how close she stands?

Yes, and the study of this fascinating subject is known as proxemics. All animals have a personal space, and so do humans. Anthropologist Edward T. Hall coined the word proxemics to define the study of personal space. In *The Hidden Dimension* he describes four divisions of space for North Americans: public distance (about 12 feet) for impersonal gatherings; social distance (12 to 4 feet) used by acquaintances; personal distance (4 feet to 18 inches) the distance we keep all others; and intimate distance (from 18 inches to body contact) for sex and lovemaking.

Animals also have a personal space, which varies from species to species. If you invade an animal's personal space, its fight or flight reaction will take over. Try this with a strange dog on the street. If you stand ten feet away, the dog will probably ignore you. But get within two feet, and it will consider you a threat. The dog will either move away or attack.

When you're on a date, the knowledge of proxemics can help you determine whether your partner wants to be kissed. Keep in mind that men's and women's intimate spaces differ. A guy's is slightly more than a girl's. You can measure your own intimate space by stretching out your arm. Your intimate space begins at approximately the middle of your forearm (a spot halfway between your wrist and elbow) and includes all the space from that point up to body contact.

In general, a girl's intimate space is shorter than a guy's. So she may think she's only standing in your personal space, not your intimate space, when in fact she has invaded your intimate space. To you, it seems like she's inviting a kiss. To her, she's just making friendly conversation. Notice this when talking to girls at parties. They like to stand closer than you do. You may interpret this as a sexual overture, but it's not.

A good rule to remember is that you're not being invited to kiss a girl unless she's so close to you that she can touch you with her elbow. If a girl gets this close, she's generally flirting with you. That's a good sign she wants to be kissed.

How can I achieve kissing fluency?

The most important thing you can do when kissing is to slow down, take your time, and simply try to enjoy the physical sensations of lip contact with someone else. A young man says, "I kissed my girlfriend for the first time last night but it was messy, tongues everywhere—we had no fluency. I want to improve my kissing so badly." If you make a conscious effort to slow down, it will certainly help. Also keep in mind how important gentleness is to a woman. Just listen to this comment from a sixteen-year-old. "When my ex-boyfriend kissed me, it felt like my lips were attached to a Hoover Power-Vac. Why do boys like to be so aggressive when most girls want to be touched (at least at first) gently, reverently, and with tenderness and compassion?" Only sixteen, and already bothered by guys being too aggressive! Be soft and gentle and she'll love you. She might even think you have kissing style.

How can I prevent awkwardness?

"When I kissed my girlfriend for the first time, it didn't go so well. It kind of happened all at once and took me by surprise. We were at school, and without warning she went to kiss me and our lips smashed together, and it was just a horrible job on my behalf. What do you suggest I do next time?"

Slow down and take your time. If necessary, gently grab her

by the shoulders so she can't get away, then take control of the kiss. Even if she initiates the kiss, you can take control midway. It's really not uncommon for lips to smash together accidentally now and then. Just think of it like two spacecraft rendezvousing in space—sometimes they come together with a little bump. But then the astronauts use their thruster controls to slow and steady the spacecraft so that they dock gently. You must use your arms in a similar way. Reach out, grab hold of her, and guide her toward you. It's usually easiest to take her by the shoulders. You could also put your hands around her back or waist. Pull her gently forward, aim your lips at hers, and go in for your docking maneuver—that is, your kiss. Execute it slowly at first. The initial kiss is bound to be the most dangerous because you could slip off or miss your mark. But it's not half as hard as docking a ship in space, so count your blessings—you don't have to go through training to do it right. You've already got plenty of training bringing food, utensils, and beverage glasses to your lips. Just aim, move slowly, and remember to hold onto her—even by the *ears* if necessary—so that you can guide your two pairs of lips to a successful docking.

Should I form a liplock?

You don't need to. It's optional. Many young people ask, "Are the lips supposed to form a lock or just stay sandwiched together while our mouths move?" Once your lips are in contact, there are no real rules. Just do whatever feels good to you and your partner. You could form a liplock, but that's not at all necessary. The best analogy I can give you is eating an apple. Sometimes your lips are locked onto it, other times your mouth and lips move over it to find a good spot. Just remember not to take a big bite out of your sweetie.

Will my partner know I'm a novice?

No. There's really no way they can tell that it's your first time or that you're new to it. In fact, your newness and excitement will probably make the experience all the more pleasurable for your partner, too, because your kisses will be fresh and spontaneous rather than rehearsed and secondhand. But they'll never know your secret unless you tell them.

How old are most people when they have their first kiss?

Most people (86 percent) experience a first romantic kiss in their early or mid-teens. But don't worry about having a first kiss later in your life. Sometimes people don't start until they're in their twenties. Even if you start substantially later, there's nothing to worry about. You can quickly catch up with everyone else—it's such an easy thing to do once you get started! Kissing earlier, like eight or nine, is fine, too. You can sometimes tell the ones who started really early. They walk around with big self-satisfied grins on their faces like they know a secret. Other times they just look shocked and dazed, as if they experienced some other-worldly contact they can hardly believe.

Does everyone get kissing jitters?

A first kiss always causes anxiety or nervousness. So you're not alone in feeling that way. Most people feel butterflies in their stomach before a first kiss. Try to relax and enjoy it. That excitement is part of the joy of being alive, so be thankful for it. When you don't feel it, the spark has gone out and you're missing out on all the fun.

Is it okay to kiss on a first date?

Yes. About 50 percent of people think so. The benefits are that it's exciting, you break the ice quickly, and you no longer have to worry about when the first kiss is going to occur. The disadvantages are that you don't have a magical first kiss to anticipate anymore, and you may find out that your new partner isn't compatible with you. I routinely hear from young people who kiss approximately one or two new people every week. Sometimes this spins their heads around so much they get dizzy trying to remember who they're going out with and who they really like. One woman had so many guys kissing her she was thinking of hiring an accountant to keep track of them. But other than these organizational disadvantages, it can be fun to kiss someone new every few weeks. Some people get addicted to the excitement of new relationships—it actually feels like a caffeine high that can last for weeks. After that, they're often compelled to move on to someone new for another romantic shot in the arm.

Is it mandatory to kiss on a first date?

No. You don't have to get intimate, although if you go on a few dates without kissing, you will almost certainly feel some social pressure urging you to kiss. But you can really wait a few dates before you do it. You can even go on five or six dates—or more, depending on your budget and imagination—without kissing.

How can I cope with the pressure to kiss?

Many young people start to feel pressure to kiss when they're in their teens. This is part of the social conditioning I mentioned in the first chapter. In a way this pressure is good, because it pushes you out of the nest, so to speak. But it can also cause anguish. For example, one young woman says, "Though I'm involved in school and have a lot of friends, I'm kind of socially retarded in the sense that I've never had a boyfriend and I'm about to graduate from high school. I'm dating someone now, and have been for a month or so. Because I'm so old and have never kissed anyone, I'm afraid to try. My new boyfriend and I have been seeing each other at least three times a week, and I think he's beginning to wonder if we're ever going to kiss. He knows how inexperienced I am, and he has told me that he doesn't care, but I'm still way afraid. What do you think about this?"

If you're happy being together, that's the important thing. When you're ready to kiss, you will. You're not unusual if you haven't kissed until your late teens. So don't buckle under the pressure. If you'd like to be kissed, tell your boyfriend that you want him to kiss you with a line like this, "Roger, it's about time you kissed me! What the devil are you waiting for, Christmas?" Or tell him that you want to kiss *him*. The best time to tell him is after a romantic date. It may help to rehearse in your imagination, planning how you'll make that first lip contact with him.

Does talking about it beforehand ruin it?

Yes, it almost always does. One fifteen-year-old says, "My first kiss was a total mess because my boyfriend and I sat around for half an hour talking about how the kiss was inevitable. The more we talked about it, the more paralyzed we both felt. We sat there looking into each other's eyes. Then I noticed he was trembling, his face got red, and tears started coming out of his eyes. When our lips finally connected, it was no fun. We had talked all the excitement out of it!" It's much better to do it without saying too much, or anything, about it.

How long should a first kiss last? And how do I know when to end the kiss?

Most kisses in the United States, including first kisses, last no longer than one minute. Now, when your first kiss occurs, you'll probably be so excited you won't be thinking straight. Your heart will be beating fast and you'll be kind of breathless. Your sense of time may be distorted. It may seem like the kiss is taking forever, when in actuality it will probably only last a few seconds. Whatever you do, don't start counting mentally, one thousand one . . . one thousand two. . . . Instead just wait until your lips have been in contact with your partner's for a few seconds. Rock your head back and forth a few times. At this point you'll probably feel slightly dizzy from excitement. Despite your mental elation, keep track of what your partner is doing. They may have their own agenda. He or she may be giving you little pecks or a gentle sucking action on your lower lip. Your partner might also try to insert their tongue into your mouth during a first kiss. This may really throw you off, but you've got to be prepared for it. (Tongue kisses are discussed in the next chapter.) Deal with whatever scenario develops and then, after a few seconds, when you feel like you're about to faint from pleasure and excitement, make a decision that your first kiss will come to an end.

The easiest way to end a kiss is to bring your lips together and gently pull back. Just before pulling their head away, some people like to give their partner a little peck on the lips, as if they're cutely saying "Bye-bye!" Another trendy way to break off is to rub your noses together like Eskimos.

Sometimes you'll be so involved in a kiss that you won't know when to end it. Your mind may be so disoriented by the thrill of lip contact that you can't think clearly. Or you may be having so much fun you don't want to stop—in which case, by all means, continue the kiss and wring every last drop of pleasure you can from it.

On the other hand, you might feel that you would be insulting your partner by breaking off. Have you ever been to a party and gotten into a conversation with someone and not known how to break away and stop talking to them? Well, if this happens during a kiss, just make a mental decision to break off, close your lips, and gently pull back. Smile at your partner as if to say, "That was fun—maybe we can do it again sometime."

Should I ask before I kiss?

Not usually. Instead, *demand* a kiss with the line from Shakespeare's *The Taming of the Shrew:* "Kiss me, Kate!" Say something like that, but in a gentle, loving voice. (And remember to change the girl's name unless you're dating a Kate.) Or say, "I'd like to kiss you." Better yet, just wait for the right moment. Say nothing—make your move when the time is right.

This advice about not asking works best for 90 percent of people. But a small percentage do like to ask first. One guy told me that asking always worked for him. "Can I give you a kiss?" was his line, and he had plenty of luck with it. So, if you're in that 10 percent, be polite and ask away.

Is it okay to wait for the other person to make the first move?

Sometimes that's the best strategy of all; in fact, it can also be the most romantic. Talk with your date in the street as you walk together. Go to his house, visit his family, then talk to him alone. Little by little you'll build up such romantic expectations that both of you will be dying for a kiss. Go to the bathroom and check yourself in the mirror. Hair still in place? You look great! Go back to him and continue flirting. Give him a little compliment . . . wait for him to laugh—his smile seems to be inviting you. Now you're standing together looking into each other's eyes. Restrain your impulse to lean forward and kiss. But do get closer. If necessary, make some excuse for your move—straighten an article of his clothing, flirtatiously brush his hair aside, or tell him you want to smell his cologne (if he's wearing it).

If your date sits on the couch, follow his example. This is called mirroring. You do what he does. If he laughs, you laugh. If he crosses his legs, you cross your legs. Most lovers find that this happens automatically. It's like you're falling into a trance. You'll find yourself being drawn toward him with an irresistible force. Go with the feelings. Keep things light and upbeat. Before you know it, he'll make a move. Be prepared for it to happen. If he leans forward for a kiss, help him out. Mirror his action—lean forward and kiss him back. It may look like he initiated it, but he couldn't have done it without your help. You actually did more than half the work just by being there, mirroring him, and getting close! And congratulations, girlfriend, you've just redefined the term *passive-aggressive.*

How do I kiss on Valentine's Day?

If you're planning to kiss a girl for the first time on a special occasion, such as Valentine's Day, you should still keep in mind everything I said about building up the romance and waiting for the right moment. On a special occasion, this romance is always in the air. The very fact that you got together on that special day should add to the excitement and togetherness you'll feel.

Give her flowers or candy before your Valentine's Day kiss and observe how she reacts. Does she smile? Is she happy? Does she seem to enjoy your company? Keep escalating the romantic attraction between you by complimenting her and getting close. See how she reacts to this, too. In a music store, for example, hand her a CD. Stand a foot away from her when you give it to her. Let the sound of the music in the store enhance the moment. As she looks at the picture, look at it with her. Point to something on the cover—and as you do, you'll be so close to her that you might even feel . . . the *heat* from her face on yours. This will usually be enough to take your breath away. Gather your wits about you. When she hands it back to you, let your fingers touch hers. Do you feel that jolt of electricity? Do you think she felt it too? Then lean forward and close the circuit! Kiss her then and there—

Are you sure this is the right—

—yes, kiss her in public!

Let the world know you love kissing her!

The basic moves are always the same: wait until it's romantic, move closer, connect. If she retreats at any point, go back and start at the top. Sometimes this game can go on for hours, days, weeks . . . years! Ah, the trials and tribulations of love! How frustrating it can be! And, oh, how sweet it is!

How do I get close enough to kiss without telegraphing my intentions and getting rejected?

You're in the glee club office at school, just the two of you. You've been talking, and the situation feels special and romantic. The only thing that remains to be seen is whether you can get close enough for a first kiss. She's sitting on the desk, her feet gently swinging above a stack of programs. Look at her and smile. If she smiles back, go over to her and pick up one of the programs. Glance at it, then hand it to her, commenting on it. When she looks at it, sit beside her on the desk. When she passes it back to you, compliment her on her hair. No matter what it looks like, say something nice about it. She's staring at you now, her face turned toward you. It seems like the light of the setting sun has burst into the room, bathing her in a radiant glow. She's smiling like a saint. But you feel like a sinner because you have only one thing on your mind—a kiss! You've gotten yourself close enough to kiss her, now the only question that remains is—

How do I move in for it?

There are two strategies here, the clumsy strategy and the suave strategy. Let's begin with the suave strategy. In this scenario, you try to do everything right. Touch her hair or say something nice about how she looks. This will help you get close enough for the kiss. Then you lean forward, close your eyes, and press your lips to hers. The problem with the suave strategy, of course, is that things don't always go right—especially for a first kiss.

Which is why we have the backup clumsy strategy. You might as well master this one, because more than likely it's the one you'll use. In the clumsy strategy, you don't worry about being clumsy and inept. In fact, you make a conscious effort to do things the wrong way. You keep your eyes open, you snuggle up to her in an awkward manner, you bump into her with your shoulder and head when leaning forward, and your lips miss their mark the first time, landing in a crashing skid on her lower chin.

Okay, she starts laughing. She knows what you have in mind. Now she's on your side, she wants to help you. Which is the beauty of the clumsy strategy. She knows that it's not easy for a guy to initiate a first kiss. So she's going to help you through it. She turns to you and puckers up, ready for you to kiss her again. This time get it right! Now that she's primed and prepared for the kiss, sitting pretty, really waiting for it, you can hit your mark just like Cupid!

The clumsy technique is a sure bet in almost any kissing situation. The main beauty of it is that it disarms your partner and makes her realize that she doesn't have to be perfect either. This relaxes her and makes for a much more enjoyable first kiss for both of you.

CHAPTER THREE

The French Kiss

What is a french kiss?

No words can do it justice. So let me apologize right at the outset for even attempting to define it. When I say a french kiss is a
kiss in which you touch tongues, remember that definition
leaves out all the dizzying electric feelings two lovers experience
when they do it. Better to say a french kiss is magic and leave it
at that. Better to say it's a kiss in which two lovers merge their
souls. Better to say it's a kiss you can't forget, especially if done
skillfully—or unskillfully! In short, it's the most popular kiss in
the world. And for almost 50 percent of boys aged nine to
twenty-two, it's the *only* kiss they'll ever do, aside from a lip kiss.
But despite its popularity, it remains the single most misunder-
stood kiss, the one that arouses the greatest curiosity in young
people, the one that brings them closer than any other kiss, yet
the one that drives them further apart when done without finesse. Which is why I'm going to spend a little time talking
about it here. But I freely admit that what I've done is the equivalent of telling you that a roller coaster is a train ride up and
down a ramp. That dictionary definition leaves out all the ex-

citement, the thrills, the fun, the scariness. But every one of those emotions—and plenty more—await you every time you touch tongues and try your own french kisses.

Exactly how do I do it?

Okay, let's start with the basics. French kissing involves tongue contact and, like eating, there's really no right or wrong way to do it. Sometimes both tongues explore simultaneously, sometimes just one. Sometimes the guy starts, sometimes the girl. There are countless different variations, but it's easiest if you just open your mouth while kissing and see what happens! Treat the inside of your partner's mouth just like it was the inside of yours—explore, swipe your lover's teeth, search around, have some fun. Don't do anything in his or her mouth that you wouldn't do in your own. If you get bored with a movement or activity in your own mouth, you don't continue it, do you? No, you just stop. So when you get bored or tired, just stop and try something else.

You might find it helpful to think of it like eating—because they both involve oral pleasure. You know how eating some foods feels extremely good? Well, french kissing should feel the same way. Just remember not to devour your lover!

Why is it called a french kiss?

The term french kiss came into the English language around 1923 as a slur on French culture, which was thought to be overly concerned with sex. (The French retaliated, calling a condom *une capote anglaise,* an English hood/bonnet.) In France it's called a tongue or soul kiss. The term french kiss is used a lot more by teenagers than adults, probably because teenagers do it more than adults.

How do I start?

The best way to begin is with a diversionary lip kiss. During the lip kiss, slowly open your mouth. Here is where most people lose heart and get nervous. Don't worry if your pulse races crazily. It's natural to feel excited at a point like this. How strange it feels to be kissing with an open mouth! How strange and how beautiful! Your partner is likely to mirror your action and open his mouth, too. If not, then try sucking on one of his lips. That might get him to loosen up. When he opens his mouth, all you need do next is start to use your tongue.

What should I do with my tongue?

Don't be shy. Extend your own tongue—and meet him halfway. That's the courteous thing to do. And when your tongues meet, don't be surprised if your blood pressure skyrockets. You can feel your souls merging as the tip of your tongue meets and flirts with his. How soft and how sublime! It makes your heart pound, your palms sweat, your body shake. It makes you laugh, sweat, and cry all at once! Oh, why didn't I ever try this before? How could I have waited so long to do it! I was born to french kiss!

Is it dangerous?

Many guys are terrible french kissers and nearly choke and suffocate their girlfriends. Says one young woman, "My boyfriend sticks his tongue too far down my throat. Sometimes it's like I can't breathe, he gives me so much tongue." Unfortunately, some women suffer in silence, letting boyfriends nearly asphyxiate them with a kiss that's supposed to be the highest expression of love! Don't let this happen to you. There's a very easy way to ensure that a french kiss is never dangerous. The first thing to do when your boyfriend gives you too much tongue is to bite his tongue. Yes, actually bite into it like it was a bologna sandwich. That will teach him a lesson he won't soon forget.

Is biting another tongue fun?

It can be. Many people bite their own tongue when they're nervous or hungry. The technique is to gently clamp the teeth down over the tongue and then run the tongue along the chewing surfaces of the teeth, almost as if you're testing to see how sharp they are. If you do this gently enough, it can really feel good. Your partner may have to get used to it, but when he or she does, it could turn out to be one of your favorite kissing techniques because it requires a kind of loving give and take and a fair amount of trust. In fact, french kissing almost always builds trust in a couple. Because after the kiss, you'll unconsciously be saying to yourself, Hey, he could have bitten my tongue clean off, but he didn't! *Thank God!* I can really trust this guy . . . at least with my tongue.

Can I suck his tongue?

Despite how silly it may sound at first, you can even try sucking your partner's tongue during a french kiss. This can be tricky, though, because his tongue is liable to be fast, slippery, and hard to get hold of. But if you act quickly and time things right, you may be able to get your lips around his tongue just as he inserts it into your mouth. If you miss the first time, try again, pulling on it forcefully and adding some vacuum power. Treat it like a straw from which you're drinking a milk shake. Says one girl, "I regularly sucked my last boyfriend's tongue and we both thought it felt fantastic." You may have to pull your partner close with your arms so that he doesn't back away in shock and surprise.

But once he learns to relax, you can suck his tongue in a kind of pulsating action for quite some time. Don't worry if this strikes you as incredibly infantile behavior. It certainly is, but that's precisely why it's so much fun.

What is the purpose of french kissing?

People do it because they want to enjoy a kind of closeness that's only possible when two tongues are touching. Freud says we french-kiss because we're at the mercy of an unconscious drive to be reunited with our mother. Otto Rank says we french-kiss because we want to master our birth trauma. Karl Marx says we french-kiss because we're being exploited by bourgeois capitalistic propaganda. Buddha says we french-kiss because we're merging with the godhead. I think he was closest to the truth. The real reason we french-kiss, and the reason they call it a soul kiss in France, is that it makes you feel like your soul is merging with your partner's.

What goes through a girl's mind when she french-kisses?

Does he like me? Does he really care for me? Does he like the way I kiss? What's going to happen if we both get out of control? It's nice to see how turned on he's getting. And it's about time he kissed me! . . . Oh, no, he's giving me too much tongue. I can hardly breathe! Help! I feel like I'm suffocating! No, wait, okay it feels great again, that's better, that's nice, oh, yes, that's it! . . . I hope we can do this all night.

What goes through a guy's mind?

Wow, this is freaking excellent! God, what a nice mouth this girl's got. Feels like the inside of a peach! But where's her tongue? Where's her gosh-darned tongue? Is she hiding it somewhere? I'm going to find that tongue. If I don't find it in the next fifteen seconds, I'm going to stop and ask her if she hasn't swallowed it . . .

Oh, here it is! Her tongue feels sweet. It tastes nice, too. Why is she wiggling it back and forth like that? Maybe I'm supposed to do the same thing. Here I go. Let's see how she likes this. Next I'm going to lick her teeth and give her a thorough oral exam. Oh, fine! She's got braces, and they feel excellent . . . I wonder what it would be like to be married to her.

Why doesn't he know any other way to kiss?

Lots of guys have limited imaginations when it comes to kissing. They hear their friends talking about french kisses all the time, and they think, if I don't give this girl some tongue, she'll consider me a wimp. And unfortunately most guys aren't turned on enough by simple lip kisses to do them for very long. They need something more exciting, so they invariably go on to french kissing. Also, they see it as a way to escalate things to the next level (and the next . . .)

How can I tell my boyfriend to stop?

"Honey pie, sweetie cakes, listen, I have something to tell you."
   "Yeah?"
   "Well, when we're together and we're you know . . . when we're making out and kissing and all—"

"What about it? . . ."

"Well, I kinda like the way you kiss me at the outset, when you're nice and gentle and give me feathery lip kisses."

"Oh, yeah?"

"Yeah, I really like that."

"No joke?"

"I'm serious. And in fact I like it so much that you know what?"

"What?"

"Sometimes that's all I want to do."

"That's *all* you want to do?"

"Yes. If you'll just be there for me with your sweet lips, that's enough for me."

See, the strategy here is not to tell him something negative at the beginning. Instead, begin with a compliment about the kisses you *do* like. Then slip your complaint in quickly, and sugarcoat it at the end with another compliment like "You've got such soft lips!"

How can I get him to use his tongue more?

- When you're not kissing, explain how much you love it.
- Go to romantic movies, and whenever you see a french kiss, whisper to him, "Oh, I like that!" "That looks like fun!" or "We've got to try that tongue kiss!"
- Make him read this chapter.
- Train his oral imagination by talking with him about how good it feels to eat. The easiest time to start such a conversation is when you're dining together and he's eating his favorite food.
- Buy him candy and encourage him to suck it and enjoy the

taste, texture, and feel of it. Kissing is similar, but you don't have to say this.

- Make him eat mashed potatoes.
- Encourage him to drink from the same glass as you.
- Try to get him to regress in other little ways. Baby him. It may seem like he'll resist this, but keep at it. Deep down all men are babies.
- Get him to pass a piece of candy from his mouth to yours.
- Eventually get him to take candy from your mouth.
- Encourage him to initiate tongue contact by giving him only the littlest bit of tongue when kissing. See if he'll mirror your behavior. You may be giving him too much too soon. Try to get him to take the lead by backing off yourself.
- Compliment him any time he does what you like. Even pigeons respond to this kind of positive reinforcement, so I can almost guarantee that he will succumb!

Does this advice really help?

Yes, and to prove it to you, I'll let one of my readers speak for himself: "Thanks a lot for the advice in your [first] book. I tried some different things mentioned in the chapter about french kissing, and my girlfriend is now praising my kissing. I asked her the other day if she liked the way I kissed, and she replied with: 'All I can say is: Wow!!!!' She told me that if I didn't believe her, I could kiss another girl and see what her reaction is. I don't think I should try that one with her around! Thank you so much, and I hope that you'll be able to help others like you helped me!"

How can I get my partner to be creative?

Lack of creativity in french kissing is a frequent complaint. Says one young woman, "How can I get my boyfriend to put some more finesse into french kissing? His lips and tongue feel like cardboard." The best way to do this is to encourage him to mirror your behavior. Start by giving him just a little lick with the tip of your tongue. Do this to the tip of his. Then pause. Repeat the action after a few seconds. Keep pausing and repeating the action until a light goes on in his brain and he realizes that he should do the same back to you. Little by little he should follow your lead. This mirroring action is one of the best ways to train someone to do what you like. If all else fails, bring the subject to his attention when you're not kissing.

What creative things can I do with my tongue?

Explore his mouth, lick his tongue, touch the inside of his mouth, run it along his teeth, play chase with his tongue. When touching his tongue, start by using the very tip of yours. Sometimes it's fun to just touch the tips of your tongues together, then flirt with your tongues—*flirt, flirt, flirt, flirt, flirt!* quickly flicking the tip of your tongue like a little whip. Another thing you can try is rubbing your tongues together like they do in the Trobriand Islands (for more on the Trobriand Islands kiss, see pages 117–18). Ultimately, though, this question is like asking, "How should I use my tongue when eating?" There are almost an infinite number of things you could try! The tongue is the most flexible part of the human body, and what it can do will surprise you.

Should we use our tongues simultaneously?

Yes. Most french kisses are started by one of the partners, so at the outset only one tongue is being used. For example, you're kissing your boyfriend and you want a little more excitement, so you push your tongue gently into his mouth. You wait there, resting it on his lips, until he meets you with his tongue. Contact! Taxi! Takeoff! This is the handshaking part of the french kiss. Now both tongues are in the game and you begin to play in earnest. You retreat, he follows. He retreats, you pursue. Back and forth you go, and where you end up . . . nobody knows!

Can I put pressure on his tongue?

Feel free to put as much pressure on his tongue as you would put on your own. It's especially fun to push with your tongue when he gives you some resistance. It shows him you're strong. Then you can wait to see how he reacts. Does he push back? Does he withdraw? Does he start to fight with his tongue? His reaction can tell you a lot about how he's feeling. One woman said, "The way my lover frenched me gave me a good indication of how we were going to have sex." Although french kissing doesn't have to lead to sex, it can give you some idea of what kind of lover you're with.

How do I end it?

Gently withdraw your tongue to the rear of your mouth, pull back your head, and close your lips. A more abrupt method involves pulling back tongue, lips and head simultaneously. Both methods achieve the same effect—they signal your partner that you need a break. It's sometimes tactful when ending a french kiss to remain close to your partner for a moment, because quick withdrawal could be emotionally shocking. To ease the shock, give your partner a little smile and a love peck. You could also end with a dry kiss on the lips, cheek, or forehead.

Do some people dislike french kissing?

Yes, approximately one in three women has some form of complaint about french kissing. And about 4 percent of women just don't like it at all. A few typical comments may help illustrate their feelings—

➤ "French kissing doesn't do anything for me. Many guys have french-kissed me, and at first I tried to enjoy it, but it just doesn't turn me on."
➤ "What's so interesting about french kissing? You just get a mouth full of drool."
➤ "Why is it that I hate french kissing? Have I just not been with anyone who does it right? I absolutely hate doing it because when I close my mouth a little, he opens his, and vice versa. I can never get a nice pattern going."
➤ "I don't like french kissing. I'm sixteen, and I've only french-kissed once and I found it nauseating."
➤ "I rarely find french kissing pleasurable. Is this normal? Or is it just that I've been kissed badly?"
➤ "I hate doing it. I think it's gross no matter who I'm doing it with. I can't stand the feel of someone else's tongue on mine. It makes my stomach churn. I have never liked it, but I'm only sixteen, so maybe that will change, but I can't imagine

ever wanting to kiss someone like that. I'm not that comfortable with people hugging or touching me either, so maybe it's just the contact of other people . . . I don't know."

There's nothing wrong with these women. The simple fact is that not everyone likes tongue kissing. About one-third of women and 9 percent of guys do not enjoy it. Also, some men are not good at it, so you may have to wait for the right partner. You might enjoy it more with a guy who can put some variety into kissing. Also, it works best in certain situations or with certain people. For example, if you have a deep emotional connection, tongue contact is much more enjoyable. Another reason people don't like french kissing has to do with preferences. It's like eating—people have different tastes, and some people don't like certain foods. The flip side of the coin is that some tastes are acquired. Which simply means that *some* people who don't like french kissing can learn to like it under the right set of circumstances and with the right partner.

How can I learn to like it?

One way to develop a taste for tongue contact is to try and open your mind to it by reflecting on how much you enjoy eating your favorite foods and desserts. Do you like ice cream, candy, cookies? The next time you eat something delicious, focus on the feel and texture of the food. If you enjoy this, you should also be able to enjoy the sensation of another person's tongue. Your dislike of french kissing may also change if your partner changes. For example, you may feel differently if you're with a guy you like very much who excites you. With an exciting partner, almost anything can be fun. The more excited you get, the more you should enjoy french kisses.

Do all couples french-kiss?

No. Some couples just kiss on the lips. And it is possible to have a relationship without french kissing. If you absolutely dislike french kissing, you should tell a guy not to kiss you like that, and he should respect your wishes. Tell him when you're not kissing, because cooler heads will be more accepting of this request. He may try to expand your tastes, but if he can't, he has to live with it and accept it, just as he would live with the fact that you might be a vegetarian.

Is french kissing accurately portrayed in films?

No. And this can be very confusing to young viewers trying to learn to french kiss. For example, one woman says, "When people french-kiss on television or in the movies, they're always passionately opening and closing their mouths. When I first french-kissed, I tried imitating what I had seen and ended up biting my guy's tongue repeatedly. So when you french-kiss are you just supposed to sit still with your mouths wide open, tongues pressing together?" Movie and television kissing is rarely true to life because exterior action is all that can be shown on screen. Most film and television kisses depict more external action than is necessary. As Ronald Reagan said about movie kisses: "Kissing . . . in the old days was very beautiful. Actually the two people doing it were barely touching sometimes, in order to not push her face out of shape. You were doing it for the audience to see what in their minds they always think a kiss is. Now you see a couple of people start chewing on each other." The opening and closing motion you see in film and television french kisses is not necessary. (But it can be part of a sophisticated french kiss as long as you take care not to bring your teeth down in a full bite.) Two tongues can play with each other without any need for a sucking or biting action of the jaw and lips.

Is a lipless french kiss possible?

Yes, you can french-kiss without touching lips if both partners stick their tongues out at each other and then get close enough so that the tips of their tongues touch. At this point, you flirt with the tips of your tongues without touching your lips together. This unusual but playful variation almost always leads to more intimate kissing.

Is a tongueless french kiss possible?

No. A french kiss always involves tongue contact. In other words, the tongues of both partners touch at least once during the kiss, even if it's only for a fraction of a second. It is very important to remember this definition. It could save you quite a bit of embarrassment if your date decides to quiz you after a little kissing session: "Honey, did we french last night or was it just a tongueless open-mouth kiss?" To kiss with open mouths, keep your lips in contact and open and close your mouth. Usually this can be a lot of fun, especially if you segue into a lip-o-suction kiss now and then, which involves sucking on your partner's upper lip while she gently bites your lower lip.

Why do guys french so soon?

One of the most common complaints women have about french kissing is that guys often do it before it's appropriate or before the woman is ready or excited enough. This is primarily because guys get excited faster than girls. But no matter how often women voice these concerns, most guys never get the message. Says one girl: "Recently my boyfriend and I kissed for the first time. It was very unexpected to me. I wasn't expecting to french him the first time we ever kissed. Well, I didn't have time to react, so I felt really stupid." She had a perfect right to be surprised and chagrined. He went too fast, and he's the one who should be embarrassed, not her.

Is my fear of french kissing really about something else?

Yes. Sometimes kissing questions are inextricably mixed up with relationship questions. For example, one young man commented: "I have a girlfriend, but I don't know if she really likes me. I'm also not sure how to approach her when I want to french-kiss her. I'm always scared that the way I approach her will make her not like me anymore." Not being sure of someone's feelings can lead to confusion about how to kiss. In this case, the real confusion stems not from a technical kissing question but from being uncertain whether he and this girl are right for one another. Unfortunately, sometimes you can't tell until you kiss, and sometimes even that doesn't tell you.

Here's a terrific kissing secret that very few guys know: If you let your girlfriend initiate french kissing, she'll appreciate your patience, respect you, and consider you a very romantic kisser. The question is, can you wait? If you're not sure of her feelings, then you're probably not that well connected emotionally yet. If that's the case, she probably won't appreciate a french kiss from you. Many women have said that they don't like french kisses if they don't know the guy well enough. As Thomas Carlyle, the Scottish historian and essayist (1795–1881), said, "If you are ever in doubt as to whether or not you should kiss a pretty girl, always give her the benefit of the doubt." He could very well have added, "And try to get *her* to make the first move."

How much should I use my tongue?

Not too much at the start. This advice is particularly aimed at guys, who would be well advised to listen carefully to this young woman's complaint: "When I see people kissing on television, they start off with a soft peck as they move on to a passionate french kiss. Why is it that teenagers always seem to jump right into the french-kiss part and don't seem to care about the soft kiss? All of the boys I have kissed have just wanted to stick their tongue down my throat and do not have any feeling in it. Why?" Now take this little quiz, guys:

When she says a kiss does "not have any feeling in it" what does she mean?
A) She lost sensation in her mouth.
B) She must have taken an anesthetic.
C) There wasn't any heavy petting.
D) He failed to give her soft, lingering lip kisses.
ANSWER: D.

She would have preferred to get some nice soft pecks at the start—just doing that is considered a kiss with feeling in it. Write it on your heart! Listen to this advice. And you will slay her with devotion—and technique.

How should I breathe during french kissing?

During a french kiss, breathe through your nose. You can actually practice this during the day when you're not kissing. Sound boring? You'd never practice something like that? Try imagining french kissing someone you have a crush on while you practice. Trust me, you won't find it boring! By breathing through your nose, you can prolong a french kiss for many minutes without breaking lip contact. One woman complains, "My husband likes to kiss me with long, deep french kisses, but I have a problem holding my breath very long. What do you suggest?" There is no need to hold your breath since you can breathe through your nose. An alternate strategy is to interrupt him every few seconds by acting shocked, as if you just saw your neighbor walk up to your window. When your husband turns around to look, take a gulp of air. If your husband complains about your shenanigans, tell him he's suffocating you, and quickly clap your palm over his face to show him what it's like.

Why do I get nervous when french-kissing?

Because tongue contact can be as intimate as sex. It's exciting and it can lead to more advanced sexual acts, which you may or may not want. It can turn both of you on at the same time. It brings you close, and it connects you more than hugging or holding hands. And it works on your emotions. But count your blessings! That excitement means your nervous system is in excellent condition.

How can I avoid being a sloppy french kisser?

This topic is treated more fully in the sections on wet kisses (pages 84–86, 136–38), but the basic technique is to swallow your own saliva and encourage your partner to do the same. You can actually swallow during the kiss itself. Or you can take periodic breaks to swallow. You could also stop to take a drink of water every now and then. People also often ask, "Are you really supposed to swallow the other person's spit when you're french-kissing?" The answer is yes, because during a french kiss your saliva will merge, and there's no telling whose it is. Sure, this may sound messy, but the more excited you get, the less gross it will seem.

Is it done worldwide?

No. In the Arctic, french kisses are not done. In Asia, they are very rare and considered unsanitary. In the South Pacific, people usually don't start with french kisses, instead they suck each other's lower lips. Then they do a variation on the french kiss in which they suck each other's tongues and rub their tongues together. For more details, see the discussion of the Trobriand Islands kiss (pages 117–18).

Is it okay to do it on a first date?

Yes. But girls often say they don't like guys who give them french kisses too soon. So, it's usually better to wait until the third or fourth date or even longer. Then start slowly—the trick is to let her escalate it if she dares.

Should I lick the roof of his mouth?

Many guys would probably enjoy having a girl lick the roof of their mouth, but preferences and tastes certainly will vary. The more excited he is, the more likely he'll be to enjoy it. Most guys also find it exciting to have their tongue sucked and to have the tip of their tongue played with by their partner's tongue. Another exciting technique is to occasionally think of yourself as a cat and run your tongue over your partner's tongue the way a cat licks you. And most guys like french kisses that change in intensity from slow and gentle to hard and fast . . . then back again to nice and easy.

What if I have a short tongue?

Less than 1 percent of people have tongues that are shorter than normal. (And about 12 percent of people think they do but actually have tongues that are normal or longer than normal!) If your tongue is shorter than average, don't worry—tongue size is the *least* important factor in french kissing, much less important than finesse, technique, and the ability to talk about the experience with your friends the next day. First of all, your partner will never realize you have a short tongue unless you tell him. Second, you can still french-kiss adequately by concentrating on activity in your *own* mouth. And if you're a guy, girls will love you because most of them complain that their boyfriends choke them with big tongues. If you still want a longer tongue, consult your dentist for a laser procedure that can lengthen it. But the best advice is probably simply to relax and enjoy what you've got!

Do guys prefer it to closed-mouth kissing?

Most (but not all) guys prefer french kissing because when their tongues are involved it's more stimulating and exciting for them. Some men, however, (about 22 percent) prefer more romantic lip kisses. Almost all guys like a combination of french and non-french kisses. Most guys like more french kisses in the mix than girls do. The percentage varies from guy to guy, so you'll just have to observe how your partner reacts to learn what he likes.

Can't a lip kiss be just as passionate?

Yes. And if guys would just get this through their heads, the 80 percent of women who are constantly complaining about boyfriends who suffocate them with monotonous french kisses would be able to rest easier when they have a hot date lined up, knowing that their guy will kiss them romantically, like in the movies, with those tender loving lip kisses. A lip kiss is almost always much more romantic than a french kiss. A lip kiss says, "I like you honey cakes, I want to be with you, I like the look of you, the feel of you, the closeness of being with you, and I'm going to treat you like a teddy bear and hold you and cuddle you and be there for you whenever you need me, *mmmmmmmmmm, kiss! kiss! kiss! kiss!*" Whereas a french kiss says, "Honey, I like the inside of your mouth and I want to go even further." Just remember the words of one of Amelia Earhart's admirers, the American aviator who was the first woman to fly solo across the Atlantic and who subsequently crashed and disappeared in the Pacific while attempting to fly around the world: "Romance is in the lips, sex is in the tongue."

What if my girlfriend makes strange demands?

You should always do what your girlfriend wants. This is the surest way to a woman's heart. One young man complains, "My girlfriend says I french-kiss the opposite way that she likes. I asked her how she likes to be kissed. She told me that she loves to be licked *in* her lips and that I don't stick out my tongue long enough. Also that I don't touch her when I'm kissing her." All I can say is, be thankful that she told *you* her preferences instead of running off with Joe who lives down the street from her. Guys, take note! Most girls like you to touch them when kissing. Run your hands up and down her back, play with her hair, caress her face, give her a playful loving squeeze. And if you're with this particular girl, kiss her *in* her lips, just like the doctor ordered. Some of you guys must be crazy—you're not writing this down! . . . But you can bet Joe down the street is.

Should I swirl my tongue?

If you enjoy swirling your tongue around, by all means do it. Most people occasionally try this action when french-kissing. But if your partner doesn't like it, you can judge that from his reaction and stop doing it. On the other hand, if you really like it, you might be able to teach your partner to get used to it by starting out with little swirls and circles. But keep in mind that there is no requirement for tongue swirling. You're under absolutely no obligation to do it. It is a totally optional movement, like sucking the tongue, biting the tongue, exploring for little pieces of candy, or french-kissing while standing on one foot—nobody's going to force you to do it or wonder why you didn't if you don't.

Why do some guys avoid tongue contact?

About 3 percent of women are puzzled by the fact that their lover boys, contrary to the prevailing trend, avoid tongue contact. For example: "One night we were coming home from the movies. This was the night we became sexually involved. During the act of french kissing, he was not using his tongue, and I felt I was kissing a hole in the wall with my tongue. What reason would he kiss me without tongue action?" The answer is that a guy may be inexperienced, shy, or just not know that he can use his tongue. But another reason is a deeper psychological one. Sometimes a man can get into a frame of mind that is rather passive. For whatever emotional or psychological reason, he may want his partner to take the lead. Says one young man, "When I'm kissing my girlfriend, I just don't know what to do with my tongue. It's to the point where I just want to kiss not using any tongue. I know she likes to french kiss, but I can't help feeling goofy and inexperienced whenever I try." Some girls find guys like this a pleasant change of pace, giving them the opportunity to explore their own aggressive side.

What's the difference between making out and french kissing?

Making out is a general term that means kissing of any kind that also involves caressing your partner. To put it mildly, it's to die for! Any time you french-kiss, you're also making out as long as you touch your girlfriend or boyfriend's body. Making out without kissing is technically known as petting, which involves running your hands over your partner in a loving way. I don't think I have to spell out the details—it's the kind of touch that speaks for itself.

What irks women most about french kissing?

Guys, there are three things that give french kissing a bad name among women: fish-mouthing, making them gag, and drooling.

> *Fish-mouthing.* This means you're sucking on your girlfriend's lips and mouth as if you were a fish gulping for food. All hu-

mans are capable of doing this—it's an innate response. But as an adult, it's only appropriate when you're sucking on a soft-serve ice-cream cone. If you want to know how silly it looks, just observe a baby sucking on a bottle. How would you like it if your lover was doing that to your face? But in all seriousness, don't ever fish-mouth your girlfriend. The only exception is if she does it to you first or if you want to try something totally gonzo and different for a fraction of a second as a joke.

- *Making her gag.* Some guys stick their tongue into their girlfriend's mouths as if they were trying to plug a leak in a dam. If this sounds familiar, you may want to reconsider putting your tongue into her mouth at all for a while. Slow down, cool your heels, and take a break from tongue action. Your tongue may be too big for her dainty little mouth. Give it a rest. Instead, just tease her with the tip of your tongue now and then, trying to trick her into inserting her tongue into your mouth. Make that your goal over the next few weeks, and she'll love you for backing off and giving her some breathing room.

- *Drooling.* This is the biggest offender of all. You've got to learn to stop the flow of saliva from drowning her. The best way to do it is to swallow your own spit. And it's best done at least once a minute during a french kiss. You might want to try not to get *any* saliva from your mouth into hers. Admittedly that's an impossible task during a french kiss, but having that as your goal will go a long way toward making your kisses more pleasurable for her. Just lean back now and then and swallow. That's all there is to it.

Should we french-kiss every time?

No. Because sometimes you need a change of pace. There are over twenty-five other types of kisses you can try. If you french-kiss every time, you might find that you get tired of it after a while. Also some couples, and many women, say that it's sometimes more exciting to just do sweet innocent lip kisses.

Do most people prefer repeated patterns of tongue movement, or a more spontaneous go-with-the-flow type of french kiss?

Patterns are okay some of the time, but spontaneity and adapting yourself to the situation is usually preferable. About 3 percent of people approach french kissing as if they were working on an assembly line, with a regularly repeated set of tongue movements that is so monotonous and repetitious it almost drives their partners insane. Watch out if your kissing partner won't break his patterns and be flexible for you. If you're going out with a very pattern-oriented french kisser, you can sometimes help them relax by being very loving—or by getting them into psychotherapy.

What if I freeze when french-kissing?

This is a reaction some people get when they have so much pent-up energy that they don't know what to do with it. The key to unfreezing yourself is to realize that you have a lot more aggressive capacity than you realize. Try to take the lead in kissing. Remember you don't have to be passive. Move your tongue around, too. In fact, it may help if you actually try to fight with your tongues. I think this may snap you out of a kind of paralysis you've slipped into. Sometimes it's nice to be passive and agreeable. But you can't go through your whole life that way. After all, it's only a tongue. It can't hurt you! If necessary you can even bite it! One trick to develop your assertiveness (suggested by psychologist Fritz Perls) is to bite aggressively into apples. Try that exercise; it may help you unfreeze yourself when kissing, too.

How wide should I open my mouth?

You know how the dentist says, "Open wide!" and then he looks into your mouth with the mirror, and then he gets a frustrated look on his face and grumbles, "Wider!" but then you open it so wide that he can't get in because your lips aren't relaxed enough—and he asks you to loosen up a bit and actually *close* your mouth a little? Well, french kissing is the same way; sometimes a little less (openness) is more.

What is playing chase?

When french-kissing, one person often plays the lead most of the time. But you may find that it's even more fun when you switch back and forth between following and leading in an alternating rhythm also known as playing chase with your tongues. When you french-kiss like this, with a subtle interplay of control and teasing between you, you're likely to lose track of time and forget where you are completely.

How long should a french kiss last?

Thirty seconds to five minutes. Most people french-kiss for no more than sixty seconds. But a really good french kiss will last from three to five minutes, the lovers breathing through their noses during the kiss to prolong the contact, entwining their tongues, getting lost in the tingling sensations and shocks that seem to run through their nerves and over their bodies, feeling the world start to spin around them as if they were on a carousel. A rule of thumb to keep in mind is that a good french kiss should last long enough to make you a little breathless, a little excited, and a little sick to your stomach.

How do I tell my boyfriend I'm not ready?

Tell him tactfully. You must get him a copy of my first book, *The Art of Kissing,* and instruct him to try the simpler kisses first! A man who really cares will jump at the opportunity to try some new kisses with you, and there are plenty that are less intimate than tongue kisses—like ear kisses, neck kisses, upside-down kisses, vacuum kisses. Well, maybe you better hold off on the vacuum kisses for a while. . . .

Are there any other tricks to help get my girlfriend to french-kiss me?

Here's a fun (and sweet) one: First buy about twenty packages of bubble gum. Then when you're on a date, start chewing the gum and handing her one piece after another. Before long you'll each have five or six pieces in your mouth, you'll be chewing slowly, and it will feel sweet and delicious. You'll both be so focused on the chewing pleasure that you'll being to regress. Soon you'll experience the symbiotic closeness that can only come when two people are on the same wavelength. This is the best training for kissing pleasure there is. Keep chewing, looking into her eyes, and moving closer. Before long you'll feel like your mouths are connected. Your next step is to simply remove the gum from your mouth and tell her to do the same. Lean so close that you can feel the heat from her face and smell bubble gum on her breath. But now a simple kiss won't satisfy her! She'll want more! And when you start kissing she'll almost immediately seek out your tongue as a substitute for that gum, and voilà! You'll be french-kissing. For a fun variation—not for beginners—leave the gum in your mouth while kissing. Keep it to the side of your tongue when you french-kiss and see what develops.

Should I press hard against her lips?

Not at the outset. Start soft and gentle, really nice and feathery. But then after a while, you can begin pressing harder with your lips and tongue. The important thing is to vary the pressure. Try to keep your lover guessing. Try to kiss like music—sometimes loud, sometimes soft, sometimes fast, sometimes slow. The greatest compliment you can receive as a lover is when your partner says, "I never know what you're going to do next!" Change and variety are the heart and soul of kissing, so keep her guessing!

What are the exact steps in french-kissing?

- Step one is a gentle, closed-mouth kiss.
- Step two is to open your mouth while kissing and see what happens. If nothing happens, try to gently push your tongue between her lips.
- Step three is to withdraw your tongue and see if she responds. This is the most important step, and the one most guys forget.
- Step four is to test the waters again with a little tongue.

- Step five is to back away once more and watch how she responds. Again, most guys omit this step.
- Continue in this fashion until your tongues meet. Have fun, but always see how she responds and base your next move on that. She'll love you for being so attentive to her responses.
- Then once you start, it's give and take from there, playing with each other's tongues until you feel your blood pressure rise and your heart race.

Can I spice up french kissing with a certain kind of taste?

Yes. Try drinking iced tea or something that tastes good before french-kissing your boyfriend. He'll be able to taste it in your mouth. Then he drinks something different, and you get to taste it in his. You can also try it with different flavors of ice cream, which adds a cold sensation to the tongue that many people find exciting.

Should it feel like fireworks?

Yes. If you love someone and you french-kiss him or her, the feeling is indescribable. Young people have also said it makes their head dizzy, their heart pound, and their knees tremble. Your palms will begin to sweat. You'll get goose bumps, and you may feel like you're spinning out of control. You'll get breathless and feel your blood pressure go up, up, up until you think it's going to kill you. It's a lot like being in a terrible car crash, only it's not terrible and no one gets hurt!

CHAPTER FOUR

The Most Exciting Kisses

Which kisses do women find most exciting?

The most surprising finding of my kissing survey is that of all the places women like to be kissed, their favorite spot, aside from the mouth, is the neck. Every guy who's reading this paragraph should highlight the next sentence (I already underlined it for you). <u>Women like neck kisses ten times more than you do.</u> Why is unclear. All I know at this point is that neck kisses drive women out of their mind. "It makes me crazy!" is a typical reaction. At colleges, all I have to do is ask, "Gals, what is your favorite spot to be kissed, aside from the mouth?" and the majority of them usually yell back "The neck!" What can I say? If you're a guy and you're not kissing her neck, you're risking your own neck—romantically. The statistics speak for themselves. More than 97 percent of women report that they are turned on by neck kisses.

What is the best way to kiss her neck?

One woman gave the answer when she said, "To have a guy come up behind me, breathe on my neck, bite me, and kiss me there is to send a thousand volts through my spine." This is exactly what a guy should do. Brush her hair aside, breathe on the back of her neck, bite her gently, and kiss her there. She'll melt in your arms.

How else should I kiss her neck?

Start with her mouth, then after a few ordinary kisses, move down and gently kiss her neck. Then back up to her mouth. After a while, move down to the neck again, and kiss under her chin and at the side and back of her neck. Notice how she reacts; that's the most important thing. If she looks bored, try something else. But typically a woman will begin to squirm around or almost go into a trance when you kiss her neck.

What do women say about neck kisses?

"It drives me wild!"

"Makes me nuts!"

"I get shivers all over my body when he kisses my neck."

"I like the tickly, passionate feel of someone's teeth nuzzling my neck, their little sucking movements, everything!"

"I go crazy when he kisses my neck. *That* is very sexually arousing to me."

"When my boyfriend kisses my neck I get shivers all up and down my body. The same thing happens when he kisses my ears, but even more so when he kisses my neck."

"Once I was driving when he kissed my neck, and I almost fainted and had to pull to the side of the road, I got so excited."

What should I do when my boyfriend kisses my neck?

Show him how much you enjoy it. You might gently pull his hair. Talk to him, if you can. Tell him you're in seventh heaven. Squirm around. Say things like, "What are you *doing*!" Feel free to laugh, if you like. Enjoy it!

Do guys like to be kissed on the neck too?

Not nearly as much as girls. But sure, they do like it—most of them, anyway. In fact 90 percent of men *like* neck kisses. It's just that virtually none of them *raves* about it the way women do.

Do guys like ear kisses?

Yes. One young woman comments, "I have found that they really like it on their ears. If you place the tip of your tongue behind the earlobe, in the little groove where your jaw and ear meet, and probe (kind of pulsate) with your tongue, they go nuts! Girls like it just as much—at least I do."

Do women like ear kisses?

Oh, yes! Any guy who neglects his girlfriend's ears (and neck) is missing a terrific opportunity to excite her with a very simple kiss. In fact, women like being kissed on the ears about twice as much as guys. One young woman says, "When I told my boyfriend to kiss me on the ears, he reacted like I was crazy. I told him I really liked it, but since he didn't, he assumed that I didn't as well. I really, *really* like being kissed on the ears. Do I have to tell him it drives me up the wall (which it does)? Do I have to say it makes my knees weak and my stomach do flip-flops and my skin crawl with excitation (all of which it does)?" Guys, get the message? Not only do more women (94 percent) like ear kisses more than men (87 percent), but their reaction is typically much greater and more intense.

What is the best way to kiss someone's ear?

First kiss the big outer part of the ear. Then kiss the earlobe. If you want, you can gently bite the earlobe and even suck it. But most important of all, remember that when you kiss the ear, you're exciting her with auditory as well as tactile stimuli. No matter how quietly you kiss her ear, there will be some sound produced by contact with her outer ear. To this you can add the soft romantic whisper of your breath. You can also add romantic nonsense such as, "Oh, honey, you're standing on my foot." Seriously, anything you say (even mundane things like, "Did you pay the rent?") will be exciting to her. Because close proximity exaggerates the sounds and adds a whispering effect to them. The warmth and smoothness of your lips will also excite her. There is virtually nothing you can do wrong at this point except talk in a normal tone of voice—which would sound too loud. Be careful not to damage her eardrum by making any sudden LOUD NOISE. But whispers and coos, nonsense syllables like "mmmmm! . . . ooooooh!" or anything similar will be fine. She'll like any kind of baby talk too. Whatever! That's why they call these phrases sweet nothings—they mean nothing but *love*! It's all in the sound. And only by getting up close and whispering it in her ear will you achieve these results. It's a foolproof technique!

What if I feel silly doing an ear kiss?

You'll only feel silly during the first second or two as you start to do an ear kiss, because immediately after you start, you'll see how she reacts, and you'll get such positive feedback from her reaction that you'll realize the silliest things are often the nicest. Be silly. She'll love you for it.

What is a frog kiss?

A kiss popular with California teens, which may be moving eastward soon, is the frog kiss. Reports just in from students who have heard about or tried this say it involves touching tongues quickly like a frog after a fly. And once they do about twelve frog kisses, they make out. The chief value of a kiss like this is that it lets you get to know your partner during a fun game because you're eyeball-to-eyeball during the kiss. Obviously it's one of the most exciting kisses because it's so different and it almost always leads to a romantic encounter.

What is a biting kiss?

Like its name implies, it's one in which you *gently* and playfully nip your lover during a kiss. Typically this is done to the earlobe, the lips, the tip of the nose, the chin, or other parts of the body where she's sensitive. Little love bites like this shouldn't even leave a mark on the body—they're that gentle. For advice on how to execute the kiss, observe dogs who playfully bite their owners. Even these animals know that a bite can signify playfulness when it's restrained. So restrain your aggression and bite your lover. With each bite you'll be wordlessly saying loving things to her, for a biting kiss always means "Honey, I love you so much I could eat you! But I'm not going to hurt you! You can trust me."

Why is the biting kiss exciting?

Because it demonstrates that your partner has a lot of pent-up energy—sexual energy, energy that *could* be unleashed at a moment's notice. About 78 percent of men and 84 percent of women like to bite—or be bitten—during a kiss. By restraining the bite, they're signaling that they have the capacity to do serious damage, and this is symbolic of what they could do in the sexual area as well. They're saying "I might go further! Watch out! I'm holding myself back!" How delightful this is! You know there's more to come! Your lover has all these feelings for you, and at any moment you may be the recipient of them. Which is why a biting kiss is always exciting. Says one woman, "When he bites me I know he's thinking of doing more. That, in and of itself, is usually enough to make my heart race." The recipient of the bite is also put in a playfully submissive position, which most people find curiously exciting as well. To bite . . . or to be bitten? That is the question.

Do people like to spank when kissing?

Not only do they spank, but this is *the* most exciting kiss we demonstrate at college kissing shows. It all starts when half the demonstrators kneel on stage or get turned over their partner's knee. At this point, people in the audience begin screaming with incredulous anticipation. Then it actually happens. The spankers whack their partners with a loud spank—*Ow! that hurts!*—and they kiss them *oh so very* tenderly. For some reason, audiences go wild, and so do the participants. Although only about 12 percent of people occasionally spank when kissing, about 88 percent find the concept very exciting and would like to try it.

How is a spanking kiss done?

The various steps to a spanking kiss can all be accomplished in the privacy of your home. Just make sure the neighbors don't call the police when they hear the screams of pleasure—

- Put your partner over your knee. You could also do it while he or she is lying down. The person getting spanked could be either the man or the woman. Both sexes like getting spanked, and both like dishing it out!
- No one has to remove any items of clothing.
- Raise your hand slowly . . . anticipation is half the fun. Then bring it down in a loud—
- *Spank!*
- You can use a book or paddle to get more effect.
- Try it again, but this time give them a double: *Spank! Spank!*
- *Ow! Ow!*
- After every few spanks, lean forward and kiss your partner on the back of the neck or on the lips.
- Continue in this fashion, spanking away, until your hand or your partner's butt gets too sore to take any more.
- You *must* laugh while doing this! If you take it seriously, you have the wrong mind-set.

Remember, the idea is not actually to punish or inflict injury. You're trying to have fun. After you discover how much fun the spanking kiss can be, you may also enjoy trying it while standing.

What is an elevator kiss?

Any time you're in an environment that moves gently, such as an elevator, you can take advantage of the sensation of unsteadiness with a kiss. The sudden feeling of disequilibrium you experience when going up or down in an elevator can be a real turn-on. The queasy feeling you get in the pit of your stomach is a lot like the feeling you get when you're in love. Which is why elevators should always be looked upon as romantic machines. Ride up to the top and then down to the basement, kissing along the way. It's easiest if you're the only two in the elevator; you can kiss passionately—then straighten up and act nonchalant when the door opens for the next floor. The risk of discovery will certainly add to your little adventure together. The feeling is like being on a seesaw when you reach the top and feel the pit of your stomach drop out as you start going down. That momentary sense of weightlessness will make your kisses feel strangely exciting. To psych yourself up for it, listen to Aerosmith's song "Love in an Elevator." Additional places to try elevator-type kisses are boats, airplanes, roller coasters, and amusement-park rides.

What is a teasing kiss?

You begin by telling your boyfriend or girlfriend that they can't kiss you back for one full minute—they just have to *receive* your kisses. Then you kiss your partner in the most sensual way you can imagine. All the while, the rules of this game prohibit your partner from kissing you back. They have to keep their lips sealed tightly together and not open their mouth.

When is the best time for a teasing kiss?

When you've been together a long time and the excitement is gone from kissing, this one will wake up your partner and surprise him or her with a new twist. People find the teasing kiss is just what they need after being married for about seven years or when they find themselves involved in a long-term college relationship, i.e.,—one that's lasted more than two or three weeks. One young woman says, "My boyfriend never got so excited as when I told him he *couldn't* kiss me back." The best time to try this is when you're bored or need something new to add excitement into a kiss. It's like a playful poke in the ribs—just what you need to excite or annoy your lover into being a frisky kitten again.

What variations on a teasing kiss can I try?

Tickle your lover. Try to make him laugh and open his mouth. And if he does open his mouth, scold him: "You broke the rules!" Once he knows the rules of the game—that he's not allowed to kiss you back—you're free to do anything you want. Try sticking your tongue between his lips into his mouth. Remember, he's not supposed to let you get in there, so if he opens his mouth, you're free to upbraid him. Run your hands up and down his back, hug him, pull his hair—do whatever you want. He's absolutely not allowed to kiss you back. If you use your imagination, you can really tantalize your partner and excite him in the process.

Why are teasing kisses so effective?

Teasing is a form of love. Ironically it's both a sign of affection and a form of controlled aggression. But it's underlying message is always "I care for you!" We don't tease those we dislike. It also shows you're a good sport and proves you have a sense of humor. A lover who never teases gets boring pretty fast. A tease stays in the mind for hours, and a lover will remember you all the more for teasing and then showing that you really care. Tease your lover—but don't make her cry excessively. Then kiss her with a passion that says, "Honey, I was only teasing!"

What is a grudge kiss?

Sophisticated and exciting, the grudge kiss is the most Machiavellian kiss ever devised by the mind of man or woman. You may object to the grudge kiss on moral grounds, but there's no question that it's popular with the jet set and with young people looking for quick thrills. That doesn't mean it's a kiss for everyone, however. Some would say it's a kiss for those who are in need of psychotherapy. Others would argue that it's a kiss for those who want to live life to the fullest. Without trying to settle the controversy, I offer this description of the grudge kiss taken from my latest email and correspondence with people across America. The grudge kiss is not a physical technique, it doesn't involve a weird lip position or kissing upside down, and no special tongue action is required. All a grudge kiss requires is that you be in a relationship, get your heart broken, and then go out to spite your lover by kissing someone else. You don't necessarily do this in front of your lover. In fact, it's better if you do it in private; you'll enjoy it more, according to those who've tried it. You just do it to make yourself feel better. Sometimes that grudge kiss starts a whole new relationship, one that is beautiful, good, and true. Other times it's just a temporary diversion before you return to your original love. But no matter what the outcome, all who have tried it agree that whatever else it may be, the grudge kiss is invariably exciting.

CHAPTER FIVE

The Most Unusual Kisses

What is an electric kiss?

It's a kiss in which you give your partner an electric shock when your lips touch—

ZAP!

Most people want to try it at least once because it's so surprisingly bizarre. The amazing thing about this kiss is that it apparently makes manifest what lovers feel inside when kissing someone they adore—the kinds of chemical shocks caused by psychological energy, hormones, and adrenaline. But the driving force behind the electric kiss has nothing to do with mere biological reactions! It is powered by a totally different process . . . static electricity.

How is an electric kiss done?

First shut the lights off, because if you do this kiss right, you'll actually be able to see sparks of electricity exploding like fireworks in front of your eyes. Then you and your partner should stand about three feet away from each other. Avoid chairs, tables, and walls; in fact, you don't want to accidentally brush up against *anything* that could ruin the kiss. Now rub your feet back and forth on the rug to build up a strong charge of static electricity in your bodies. While doing this, be careful not to touch your partner or any other objects, which would discharge the electric potential you're accumulating. At this point you slowly approach your partner, being careful not to touch hands accidentally. Lean forward, and as your lips close to within a fraction of an inch, a powerful electric spark should jump from you to your partner's mouth—*Zap! Crack! Pow!* If you look down, you can see sparks exploding like fireworks. And if you're quiet, you can hear the electric crackle, pop, and hum—*Zzzzzzzzsssssssst!* Like a live wire! Depending on the amount of static electricity you charged yourself with, you'll also feel a stinging shock buzzing into your face and mouth a fraction of a second before your lips touch—*Eeeeeeeow! It hurts!* But it feels so *gooooood*!

This is the same elemental force that fuels lightning and thunderstorms. It's the same force that powers electric motors and lightbulbs! You've finally gotten in touch with Mother Nature herself, so be careful! The electric kiss is sure to prove more than shocking.

How much current passes through my body during an electric kiss?

It all depends on how dry the air is, but in some environments up to 4,500 volts of electricity can be discharged within 1/6,000th of a second. Typically, a teenage girl will experience a shock of between 50 and 150 volts when kissing her boyfriend in a living room. If a shaggy garment builds up the charge—as may happen when a pretty girl removes a wool sweater by pulling it up over her curly brown hair—the shock received from kissing her may approach 1,000 volts. If both partners are under wool blankets, they may experience shocks over 4,000 volts, the kind of shocks that are often extremely painful to humans and animals. You will definitely feel and hear these powerful electric discharges, and in the dark you'll see a flash of blinding light. You may even see smoke! Kissing a handsome guy under a blanket on a winter night may actually stun you with a shock so violent that for a moment you may think you've been hit by lightning.

What is the emotionless kiss?

For many years I was puzzled by complaints from people who told me that they experienced emotionless kisses. At first I worried about how to deal with this problem, and I was often at a loss and could give them no advice. Then I heard from a young woman who said that her boring and dull kisses had changed and become warm and loving. Suddenly I realized that the emotionless kiss is actually a special kind of kiss, valuable in its own right, and not a real problem.

Most people think of kissing as a romantic, loving experience. But sometimes a kiss is not like that at all. Sometimes it's a flat and emotionless event. About 14 percent of men and women have stumbled across the emotionless kiss, usually when their mind was elsewhere, when they weren't in love anymore, or when they were going through a transition of some sort. In many ways it's a sad kiss. But the wonderful thing about the emotionless kiss is that it's also a golden opportunity to improve your kissing.

To understand this curious paradox, you have to begin with the proposition that an emotionless kiss is any kiss that leaves you cold, any kiss that hasn't got the spark of love in it, any kiss that's flat, dry, meaningless. Writers like Sartre, Kierkegaard, and Nietzsche experienced kisses like this all their lives, which is one of the reasons they became existentialists. They didn't know that the emotionless kiss could be a springboard to better kisses to come.

So don't worry if you find yourself experiencing an emotionless kiss every now and then. In fact, everyone should purposefully try to feel nothing during a kiss once in a while. The very *attempt* to feel nothing will usually free your mind and produce a contrary result. Before you know it, you'll learn to transform your most emotionless kisses into their very opposite. Indeed, you must experiment with the emotionless kiss if you want to plumb the depths of the human heart and discover the mysterious way that transformations can improve a lover's life.

But never think of the emotionless kiss as an end in itself. It is instead a stepping-stone to its very opposite. Like a caterpillar, it may look and sound ugly, but it can turn into something very beautiful indeed. Allow yourself an occasional emotionless kiss and watch how all your other kisses become the wonderful, loving, caring experiences that all lovers dream of and seek.

What is a candy kiss?

This is an extremely intimate one in which you pass a piece of candy—a Life Saver or breath mint—to your partner during the kiss. The fun lies in getting something sweeter than a tongue during mouth contact. The trick is making sure that you transfer it correctly, without breaking it up, swallowing it, or grossing out your partner. The best method of accomplishing this is to start by placing a white Life Saver on your tongue. White ensures a good color contrast with the tongue. If a guy does this in front of his girlfriend and she sees it, her resulting jealousy and greed will make her want his candy. Don't let her get it!

How should I try to get it?

You should try to get it by kissing it out of his mouth! The best part of this kiss now begins as you struggle mightily to wrest that tiny little candy from his mouth, using your lips, your teeth, and most of all—your tongue. Grab that boy by the waist . . . don't let him squirm away. Pry open his lips. *Hey!* Slip your tongue in. *Enough—!* Find that Life Saver! His mouth tastes so sweet and minty, but don't be distracted! You have a goal, a mission, an objective! Get that candy into your mouth!

He flails, he flounces, he wriggles like a snake. *Gimme that candy!* Hold on tight! Plunge deeper into his mouth, looking for that Life Saver. Can you feel it? *Where the cripes is it?* Whip your tongue back and forth, moving the Life Saver toward the front of his mouth. Wrap your hands behind his neck, pull his head forward, tilt his face toward yours, yank his head down until you feel the Life Saver drop under his tongue near his teeth—

Then . . . *scoop, scoop, scoop!*

Quickly now! Use your tongue to hook the candy! *Enough is enough!* Fish for it! Press it up against his teeth. Here it comes! Get ready to bite it out of his mouth—

If he clamps his teeth on it, you'll have to resort to force. Tickle him and make him laugh until he lets go. Or bite down hard onto the Life Saver and tug it out of his mouth. If he won't let go, defy him completely . . . bite it in half!

Where does my girlfriend like to be kissed best?

Try a sliding kiss and you'll quickly find out. In fact, the sliding kiss is the best and only answer to this question. If you want to know what part of your boyfriend or girlfriend's body is most susceptible to excitation by a kiss, this is the kiss to use. After dating for a few weeks, many young people notice that their partner isn't jumping up and down with joy anymore. So they want to heat things up; they want to find that ONE SPOT that will do the trick! They have no clue where to start. The belly button? Behind the neck? The ear? *Where?* There's actually a very easy way to find out . . . although no one but *you* can find that ONE SPOT on your partner, because it varies from person to person. But when you do find that ONE SPOT—you'll know it! And you can find it with the simple technique known as the sliding kiss.

What is a sliding kiss?

Start by telling your girlfriend to roll up her sleeves. She's got to roll up her pants legs too so that you can see her ankles. It's even better if she's wearing shorts. Then tell her to recline on a couch and put one leg up so her knee is bent. Now you kneel down and begin to kiss her like this—

Begin at her ankle . . . kiss it . . . then kiss up her leg . . . up to her kneecap . . . up and down her exposed leg you go. Kissing down her thigh, skip over her shorts—never kiss on fabric (the one exception being nylons) because you don't want to get fibers in your mouth—and push up her shirt to kiss her exposed belly, and oh! oh! oh! OH! OH!

up to her neck!

up—

up

up

Up

Slide your lips along, kissing her exposed flesh as you move . . .

Then start again, but this time begin on her hand. Kiss her hand, up her arm, up past the inner part of her elbow, executing tiny little kisses along the way. This is the key to the sliding kiss; as your lips move lightly and effortlessly across her flesh, pucker up and plant tiny little pecks, leaving a trail of kisses in your wake . . . It looks like this when you start at her foot—

```
                cap
              knee  then
          her      down
        up to      kiss!
       kiss!        kiss!
       kiss!        kiss!          oh!
Mmmm kiss!                  kiss her belly   kiss her neck!
```

How will I know when I hit that ONE SPOT?

You'll know because your girlfriend will wiggle and squiggle and hoot and holler. She'll laugh! She'll sigh! She'll moan! She'll cry! She'll flip and flop and act so silly, you'll know you're there—you'll *know* you're there!

Some like ankles so darned much! It tickles them—they think it's fun. They laugh and squirm. They can't sit still. Kiss their ankles, give 'em thrills!

Some like arms and forearms best. Kiss them there, on that soft hair. Make them scream and shout and swear!

Some act calm when kissed in church, but kiss their palms and watch them lurch!

Kiss her legs? She's not amused. But kiss her belly, she's enthused.

A man must kiss where a man must kiss, but *sliiiiiiiiide* along so nothing's missed. Smack her backside—she gets pissed. Peck her peepers? She insists!

How to know what spot gets kissed? Don't take a guess—that's hit or miss. Never guess, never lose. Kiss her stockings, not her shoes! Kiss her belly, not her shirt! Kiss her body, not her belt! Kiss her till she starts to melt. Then mark THAT SPOT with ink and pen, and come back later and kiss again.

Let him kiss you—don't be snooty. Wear a T-shirt like a cutie. Try to act a bit more lenient. Never say it's inconvenient. A sliding kiss may seem laborious, but hit THAT SPOT . . . it's so damned glorious! Tell him where it really itches—feel him kiss you in those niches. Men were made to kiss like this—the sliding kiss—

the—

sliiiiiiiiiiiiiiiiiiiding

kiss!

Help him out, be his guide. When his kisses start to slide . . . point, pull, poke, pace. He'll be kissing *everyplace.* If you like it, give instruction; orchestrate your own seduction!

Do some people like kisses in unusual places?

Do they ever! And you've got to be open-minded about these offbeat kisses. Time invested in a little kiss that you find silly could make your partner very happy and appreciative. The art of kissing sometimes involves the art of compromise, for compromise is the stuff of relationships. So observe your partner as you kiss across her body and find out where she giggles and sighs. One woman said, "I like being kissed directly in my armpit!" Don't laugh! About one person in every two thousand loves this.

What's a wet kiss?

A kiss in which a lot of slippery action takes place. Lips lock, people start kissing, and before they know it, they're so slippery they could slide off each other's face like two ducks in a pond. Sometimes this watery interaction can be fun, especially if you're excited enough to enjoy the connection with your lover even at the expense of a little sloppiness. But more often than not, people complain about sloppy kissers.

What can I do to prevent them?

Start by swallowing your own saliva. Another thing you can do is stop and take a break to drink something. Have a bottle of ice water available for you and your date. This will give you an opportunity to swallow. You could also try kissing on a full stomach—people tend to salivate less after eating. Kissing before mealtime may induce more salivation. *You look so good I could eat you!* Unfortunately the brain sometimes can't distinguish between a lover and a great meal.

How wet should a kiss be?

Although some messiness is an unavoidable part of kissing, most kisses should not leave you needing a toweling-off. As kisses become more erotic, however, they do tend to get wetter. Fortunately, as people become more excited, their tolerance for saliva also goes up. Here's a simple equation you can use (a lot simpler than the stuff they taught you in trigonometry): The more excited you get, the faster your heart beats, the more your palms sweat, and the more turned on you get—the wetter a kiss can be. For most of them, though, you shouldn't need a plastic bib.

Do people who dislike sloppy kisses have a different personality?

Yes. The squeamish seem to be less willing to let loose and have fun. They can't stand even a little bit of saliva from their partner. They can hardly stand their *own* saliva. Japanese novelist Yukio Mishima was one of the squeamish. He killed himself in 1970 partly because he was even disgusted at the act of eating—it was too sloppy for him!

If your partner complains about your kisses being too sloppy but you're just giving him a normal kiss, then he may have a hangup about saliva. Of course, the converse may be true—you may actually be drooling excessively. The only way to tell is to consult your dentist next time you go for a checkup.

Is it rude to wipe your mouth afterward?

Not really. It isn't any more rude than it would be if you were dining together. Everything in moderation. But keep in mind that wiping your mouth could be interpreted as implying that you didn't like their saliva—so do it just occasionally, as if you were in a fancy restaurant.

How can I tell him his kisses are too wet?

Mention it to him when you're not kissing. It's too confrontational to do it when kissing. Suggest that he swallow his own saliva. Point out some neat dry lip kisses you see on television and in movies. Tell him if he doesn't dry out, you're going to require that he wear a bib. Also see pages 136–38.

When are wet kisses okay?

Most people prefer short and dry to start, followed by long and dry. Only after you've been kissing for a while do people get excited enough to tolerate wet kisses, i.e., after about ten minutes of kissing you might relax a little bit about the wetness issue. Virtually no one likes to be covered in spit at the end of a make-out session either. You've just got to be careful with wet kisses. They can be erotic, but lots of people can be squeamish about them. In other words, swallow your own saliva. Watch for your partner's reaction, too. If she starts gasping like a drowning woman, wipe her off and yell: "Lifeguard!"

What is an underwater kiss?

It's a kiss done partially or totally submerged in a pool, with never a care about what onlookers may think. Fifty percent of men and women like this kiss, have tried it, or would like to try it. The underwater kiss can be accomplished by holding your breath and then taking a dip together. While underwater, press your lips to his or hers. Naturally, all the normal precautions you'd take when underwater apply, like holding your breath and not opening your mouth. The kiss can be especially erotic because the watery environment tends to make you feel closer. Some men find the view of women underwater to be especially attractive, which may account for the popularity of mermaids in modern mythology. So be his little mermaid, and kiss him underwater. (By the way, this works in the shower, too!)

What is a smacking kiss?

It may sound silly, but 75 percent of people like the smacking noises of their kisses and even get turned on by hearing them made by other people. Although one gal says, "I like the noise if it's *me* making it—I don't like listening to other couples."

To get the full benefit of the kiss, open your mind to the sounds of lips smacking, sucking, and noisily puckering. Exaggerate the noises. One tricky technique involves giving your partner a series of little pecks, each one with an exaggerated sound made by vacuuming in your breath and smacking your lips apart, so that it sounds like a staccato machine-gun burst of tender little pecks—(very fast and loud): *Smack! smooch! kiss! kiss! kiss! kiss! kiss! kiss! kiss! kiss! kiss! kiss!*

Catch your breath!

What is a music kiss?

The music kiss is a Dionysian extravaganza done to the beat of rhythmic music. But don't let that definition scare you off. It's *really* fun and easy to do.

- Put on good music. Make sure it has a driving beat.
- Get close to your partner.
- Listen to the music. On the beat you . . . kiss!
- Each time you kiss, turn your head.
- Each time you turn your head, your noses pass.
- Connect with a kiss!
- Break apart and turn your head.
- Kiss!
- Break apart and turn your head.
- Kiss!
- Turn.
- Faster and faster! And always on the beat!

Start by kissing only on the *eighth* beat. Count mentally:

"1 . . . 2 . . . 3 . . . 4 . . . 5 . . . 6 . . . 7 . . . *kiss!*"

Then kiss on the *fourth* and *eighth* beat:

"1 . . . 2 . . . 3 . . . *kiss!* . . . 5 . . . 6 . . . 7 . . . *kiss!*"

Then kiss on every *other* beat!

"1 . . . *kiss!* . . . 3 . . . *kiss!* . . . 5 . . . *kiss!* . . . 7 . . . *kiss!*"

Finally you'll be kissing on every beat, which—be forewarned—is really fast and furious kissing—

"Kiss! . . . kiss! . . . kiss! . . . kiss! . . . *kiss!* . . . *kiss!* . . . *kiss!* . . . *kiss!*"

Are there any other tricks for the music kiss?

Yes. Most beginners forget they have to turn their head after *every* kiss! And each time you turn your head, girls (and guys with long hair) should also snap their head during the turn fast enough so that their hair flips from side to side. If you've got shoulder-length hair, or longer, this looks so excellent it's an absolute turn-on to see it. It's one of the most beautiful parts of the music kiss. If you have a ponytail, it will look exquisite! Ironically, the music kiss is the most visually beautiful kiss. Be sure to do it in cars so people get jealous. (Only at a red light or stop sign, of course!)

What is a perfume kiss?

"Something smells good!"

Your boyfriend is poking around in your hair at the back of

your neck, snuffling along your shoulders like a dog on the scent, hunting for something, kissing you as he goes. And luckily you dabbed your pal Debbie's Dior perfume on your arms and neck. No, wait! On your neck you used that scented body oil, White Musk, from the Body Shop. And just your luck, this morning you were in the mood to be creative, so you used two other fragrances, Dolce Vita on your legs and Poison on your stomach. Has Chucky ever got a few surprises in store for him!

"Mmmmmm! Honey, you smell delectable!"

Delectable? You never even knew he knew a word like delectable. You hardly know what it means yourself, but you know you like the way he's rooting around down your back, as if he were going to climb down your shirt at any moment. It feels so funny—

"Oh, honey!"

"Stop squirming!"

"You smell so good down past your neck. I'm kissing you on every spot that smells good to me!"

And as he moves, the fragrance of the Poison rises gently, masking every other fragrance, drawing him into its spell—

"He he he! He he he!"

—until you can't stand it anymore, it's making you laugh out loud.

And so goes the perfume kiss, a kiss in which your scent is like a target for the kisser's nose, drawing him deeper into your web, calling forth the hound dog in a man, making animals of your boyfriends, and getting them to kiss you where you want. It's magic the way a kiss can revolve around a lovely fragrance.

What is a role-playing kiss?

It's a let's pretend kiss, one in which you and your lover pretend to be other people. Also known as a fantasy kiss, it lets you do the impossible—switch your identity, the time you live in, or anything else about yourself, for the duration of the kiss. It's temporary insanity, and it's so much fun! Some typical examples follow:

- **Slave and master.** In this role-playing kiss, one of you is the slave; the other, master. The slave must do everything the master says. This includes kissing when, where, for how long, and in what manner the master commands. The fun of the game lies in humiliating and being humiliated. Some people enjoy having complete control over someone else. Others like *giving up* complete control.
- **The androgynous kiss.** In this one you mentally switch sex roles when kissing. You don't have to change clothes or talk or act different; all you have to do is use your imagination. The nice thing about the androgynous kiss is that both of you can play simultaneously, or you can do it yourself without even telling your partner what's going through your mind. This kiss is sure to expand your appreciation of the life of the opposite sex and give you a new understanding of the other side of your psyche. About 98 percent of people, however, find this one too frightening to even consider. An excellent example of the androgynous kiss appears in the film *Belle Epoque.*
- **The gangster kiss.** In this variation of the role-playing kiss, you pretend to be criminals. Kissing while on the lam, you sneak around buildings, carry fake guns, and keep looking over your shoulder to make sure the feds aren't on your tail.

In a way it's like playing cops and robbers with your lover, only you're both robbers.

♪ **Other role-playing kisses.** Another popular role-playing kiss involves pretending you're having a secret affair. Like the gangster kiss, this kiss is fraught with danger, because you think you're going to be discovered at any moment. Some people also like kissing while their partner is wearing a mask, which can facilitate fantasizing that your lover is someone else.

You can always invent additional fantasy kisses on the spur of the moment, and by being creative you can custom-tailor them to fit your own wacky and wild relationships. After seeing a movie, for instance, you can pretend you're a character from the show—murderer, thief, seductress, even cartoon character. There's no limit to the kinds of kissing games you can enjoy . . .

"You talkin' ta me?"

What is the new hand kiss?

Most lovers think of hand kisses as formal and unexciting relics from a bygone age. Very popular in Poland, the hand kiss is still considered a mark of respect in Europe. But recently some college students have been telling me about a variation on the hand kiss they have discovered in which the girl, for example, kisses her boyfriend's fingers and then kisses the spaces between the fingers and then sucks the fingers and kisses the center of the palm. "The kiss is exciting and so different, my boyfriend had no idea what to expect the first time I did it," says one college student. "But now he loves it, and I kiss his feet like this, too."

One little-known fact may tempt you to try a few hand kisses of your own. There are more nerve endings in the hand than in any other part of the body except the tongue and mouth! This means that if you kiss your lover's hands, especially the thumb and index finger, you'll be giving him more excitement than most people ever realize. Bite the fingers gently after you warm up into the hand kiss. It may look unusual, but it's a kiss that's waiting to be rediscovered.

What is the slip-off kiss?

Slip-off kisses usually occur by accident when a lover's mouth slips off his partner's during a kiss. *Huh, what happened?* The kiss, however, can also be done deliberately for a supremely comic effect. It's one of the best ways to tease when kissing. You slip off and blame it on your lover—

"It's that lipstick you're wearing, honey!"

The slip-off kiss can also be combined with comments made in the heat of the moment. For example, slip off and say:

"I can't take it any more. We have to get married!"

"Your kisses make me dizzy."

"I need an ear test."

"Quit pushing!"

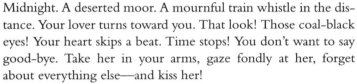

CHAPTER SIX

The Most Romantic Kisses

Midnight. A deserted moor. A mournful train whistle in the distance. Your lover turns toward you. That look! Those coal-black eyes! Your heart skips a beat. Time stops! You don't want to say good-bye. Take her in your arms, gaze fondly at her, forget about everything else—and kiss her!

Kiss her like there is no tomorrow!

Kiss her as if you were telling her you love her! Then tell her—

—with your kiss!

This is romance. And to understand the essence of romance, we must analyze each of these elements in turn, for they can all help to guarantee that *your* kisses are like movie kisses, like the kisses in romantic novels, and like the kisses in your dreams.

How can I make her pulse quicken?

Some kisses are more exciting than others. Romantic kisses always have an added factor of pulse-quickening intensity that springs from the fact that something more is happening than simply two lips or two tongues touching. What is this special energy that fuels the romantic kiss? It is connection between souls. It is a mystical, spiritual connection that goes beyond physical reality. You don't even have to be religious or mystical to believe in this power—you simply have to acknowledge that there is a chemistry of the heart that works its magic between two people. No astrological or philosophical system can adequately define what is going on. With that said, how do you achieve this magical connection?

Every romantic kiss is preceded by a conversation or at least an exchange of ardent glances between two lovers. One woman said her most romantic kiss occurred in a bar. "All night I was with a group of friends. We were drinking and laughing and dancing. But across the room, I noticed a tall, dark stranger staring at me through the crowd. At the moment our gazes met, I felt a tingle go through me." How to explain it? You can't! It's the magic of romance.

"Then as the night unfolded, every now and then I would glance in his direction, and he would always look back. I felt like he was flirting with me from across the room."

Later, when she emerged from the bathroom, he was standing by the edge of the bar. "As I came out, I saw him again. His gaze seemed to draw me toward him. We never said a word! We couldn't anyway because it was so loud in the bar. But I felt like I was being drawn to him by a magnetic force! It was incredible. My heart was racing, my blood was pounding in my ears, and I could smell the delicious scent of beer on his breath. And then suddenly he kissed me! It seemed to suspend me in time. I almost fainted. His arms went around me, and it was heaven! After what seemed like an eternity of this, I had to go back to my friends. I thought I would see him later, when things got quieter. But in the crowd, I never could find him again. Nevertheless, that was the most romantic kiss of my life—a wordless kiss exchanged between two strangers."

Again, the secret romantic element that makes the heart race is the situation the couple finds themselves in, a situation that allows them to connect on some spiritual level, either through gazes, conversation, dancing, or touch. Make sure you talk to your girlfriend in a sincere way. Catch her eye from across a room and smile at her. Touch her hand when you make a point. Stay with her in a crowded room. Connect with her on some level. All this will build expectation and reinforce your connection. The stranger-in-the-bar scenario should show you that you don't even need words to build that connection. Sometimes all it takes is a look that says "We're right for each other!"

How can I find romantic spots to kiss?

This chapter opened with a midnight rendezvous on a moor. A moor is a flat patch of ground, like a field, and you can find places like that in almost any rural area. Most city parks will also do the trick. This landscape has two elements necessary for a romantic kiss—the physical beauty of the location and isolation. It doesn't have to be the royal gardens at Versailles, as long as there's a nice tree or a fence or a view of the sunset. You get the picture—anything that you and your lover can enjoy together because of its aesthetic qualities.

Why does aesthetic pleasure heighten romance? No one knows for sure, but it certainly does. Lovers feel a special bond when they're in a beautiful and awe-inspiring place. Primate specialist Jane Goodall speculated that even chimpanzees feel a sense of awe when they watch a sunset over Lake Tanganyika.

Apes may feel awe, but probably only humans can find true romance in such a spot.

For one of the best romantic experiences of your life, try going to a museum. You don't even have to like art for this to work. Even if you can't stand any of the paintings of Van Gogh or Picasso, you'll nevertheless find it a romantic experience. Just seeing all the colors and the big rooms and the shiny floors will excite your imagination. A kiss at the end of a date in the Egyptian wing, for example, will transport you to another world.

Sometimes the physical beauty of a location will be subjective. For example, a city street on a dark night may be a dreary place, but if you look at it with an open mind, noticing the way the lights flicker across the fenders of the cars and the subtle interplay of light and shadow on your lover's face—all these visual elements can enhance your pleasure. Point these things out to your lover, and enjoy the scene together.

Why is privacy important?

In addition to a physically attractive spot, try to find one that will make you and your lover feel that you're the only two people on the planet. This is important because togetherness and specialness are two elements that heighten romantic kisses. The idea of a moor always conjures up images from the novel *Wuthering Heights.* Catherine and Heathcliff met there, alone among the barren and stark beauty of nature. In that wild playground they grew to love one another, a love that persisted even after they died!

What is the "movie set" technique?

This little trick involves imagining that wherever you are is a movie set. Treat the things in a room as props. Pretend the people are actors in a scene with you, and make believe the building is the location. As simple as it sounds, the light is the lighting. By imagining the scene is a set for a movie, you can heighten your aesthetic appreciation of the things, sounds, and lights in any location. By sharing this little secret with your lover, you will be inviting him or her into a special fantasy world where the two of you can enjoy the beauty of your surroundings and the special togetherness that actors feel when doing a scene together amidst a bustling cast and crew. Romance always involves a special fantastic transmogrification of the world, and there is nothing preventing you from viewing virtually any location as romantic.

Is a kiss on the lips more romantic than a french kiss?

Indeed it is! In almost every case, a lip kiss is tremendously more romantic than a tongue kiss. In fact, 46 percent of women complain that they don't get enough romantic lip kisses from their boyfriends. "How can I get a guy to kiss me like those romantic kisses in the movies?" is a frequent complaint. Every guy reading this paragraph should assume that his girlfriend is thinking that very thought when they're together. Don't even bother asking her if it's on her mind. I guarantee you, she'll appreciate it if you give her romantic lip kisses—gentle, tender kisses, the type of kisses you think of as "mushy, silly, stupid romantic go-nowhere, do-nothing kinds of kisses." She'll love them!

How should I kiss at my wedding?

Your first kiss as husband and wife should be one of the most romantic moments of your life. Not only will people be watching, but photographers will be recording the kiss on film and videotape, so it pays to rehearse. *Rehearse a kiss?* Certainly! You want it to be romantic, but you should rehearse so you know what you're going to do. Many couples find that if the man leans the woman back Hollywood-style and gives her a long, slow lingering kiss, it's very romantic and it also gives the paparazzi something to click away at. The key elements for the wedding kiss are pose and duration. Strike a pose. Pretend you're models. For all practical purposes, you will be. And make sure you hold the pose for at least fifteen or twenty seconds or more. You'll never forget it, and neither will your guests.

How should I kiss on my anniversary?

If it's your wedding anniversary, the answer is easy. Simply stroll up to your spouse and say—

"Remember that great wedding kiss that we rehearsed for hours? Well, honey, here it is a year (or ten years) later, and I feel the same way about you today as I did the day we tied the knot. Kiss me, sweetie!"

Then lean her back the way you did on that special day and kiss her for all you're worth.

If you're celebrating some other anniversary—say a graduation or the anniversary of your first date—recall something about the original occasion to your lover's mind and then tell him or her that you're going to kiss the way you did on that day. This little bit of nostalgia is important, for a strong relationship is like a brick wall, built one step at a time. If you take the time to celebrate with some romantic anniversary kisses, the wall will be fortified with love.

What is a butterfly kiss?

It's a kiss that's so romantic your lips never touch your partner at all! Instead, you flutter your eyelashes gently on his cheek. This kind of kiss is perfect when you want to be quiet and relaxed. Lean up to him and start batting your eyelashes. *Flutter, flutter, flutter!* When you feel those eyelashes brushing up against him, you're at the perfect distance. Keep fluttering your eyelashes, and if you're quiet, you can actually hear the sound of your eyelashes brushing him like the wings of an angel. This is by far the most romantic kiss there is.

What is an eye kiss?

Like its name implies, it's a kiss on the eyes. And although it sounds odd, 75 percent of women and 67 percent of men like being kissed on the eyes. If you want your boyfriend to know you really care for him, begin with a simple lip kiss. This calms him down and gets him in the mood. Next you gently kiss one closed eye, then the other. Finally you repeat the kiss in a little pattern . . . mouth → eye → eye.

Mouth → eye → eye.

Keep repeating it.

And for a mesmerizing effect—because half the fun of romance is the anticipation we feel when we know we're going to get something good—do the kisses in a regular, predictable rhythm, so that he starts to expect the next one. Set up a slow pattern, perhaps one kiss per second. Try to hear music in your head as you kiss him: one, two, three . . . mouth → eye → eye . . . over and over, to the same beat. After you repeat this three or four times, you'll have him slightly hypnotized—he'll be expecting the next kiss. That's when you tease him by pausing. When he pops open his eyes to look at you, the expression on his face will ask, "Huh? Where's the next kiss? Why'd you stop?"

Right at that moment, kiss him on the nose—*Bop!*

Gotcha!

When is an eye kiss appropriate?

Romantic in the extreme, the eye kiss is the perfect kiss for whenever your lover cries. It also works when someone is very sad and looks like they might be about to cry. Its greatest benefit is that it alleviates you from having to discuss the sad thing that's making your partner tearful. After all, you're addressing their sadness in a tangential way by kissing them on the eyes, almost as if you were trying to kiss the tears away.

The eye kiss can also work when you're just trying to be cute, different, and tender.

Keep in mind that this kiss is so loving and romantic that it may be *too* sweet for some lovers. If that's the case, if you find your partner can't believe you're being so kind and gentle, follow up the eye kiss with a rough kiss, like a biting or spanking kiss. Variety is one of the greatest pleasures in kissing.

What is a surprise kiss?

Out for a date, shopping in a mall together, Jason and Rhonda stop to look at some shoes. They're standing outside the window of a shop. People are passing by behind them. Rhonda leans close to look at some boots, and when she stands up straight, Jason quickly kisses her on the mouth. Surprised, Rhonda's face turns beet red! She's also a little thrilled. Because about ten people must have seen what happened. Then they walk on again through the mall, and all the while she's beaming with pride. She got a surprise kiss and it felt great!

It works virtually anywhere. You can even do it in church! And just about everyone likes to be surprised with a kiss, so you really can't go wrong.

Is there any trick to it?

Since it's a surprise, your partner may not know what you're doing and may get a little taken aback. One woman said her boyfriend, who is a police officer, has very fast reactions. As she went to give him a surprise kiss, he grabbed her in a judo hold! Then he sheepishly apologized and said he had been training so much that he reacted instinctively. Most people, however, will not give you a karate chop if you surprise them with a kiss. Quite the contrary—they'll be delighted!

When should I try a surprise kiss?

When your lover least expects it! One young woman got a surprise kiss from her boyfriend at a cocktail party, and she never forgot it. "He introduced me to another couple. And just as he told them I was his girlfriend, he kissed me right in front of them. It made me feel so special, proud, and happy. The thrill I got from that kiss lasted the entire night, and to this day I can still remember how good I felt!"

Is there such a thing as a truly platonic kiss, between friends?

Not exactly. Despite the misleading lyrics which suggest that "a kiss is just a kiss," this is almost never the case. Once you kiss, you almost always move the relationship up a notch, however slight that notch may be. Forever after, you'll stand on a slightly different footing with each other. You're now romantically involved, at least on some level. As long as you remember the kiss, you will have the possibility of picking up where you left off. So that even if the person goes on to other relationships, gets engaged, or even married, you two will always have a special connection, a special memory, and perhaps a special secret.

Which is why the friendly kiss can be tricky. There are so many complex situations that can come about once kissing is thrown into the mix. The only exception would be where, for example, a friend asks for a kiss for a really nonemotional reason. For example, one young woman in New York recently got her tongue pierced and a barbell stud inserted. A lot of her friends, both male and female, were curious about it and asked her if they could kiss her, just to feel what it's like!

Although 91 percent of women and 80 percent of men believe a kiss can remain platonic, only 36 percent have ever tried a friendly kiss on the lips. "Kissing on the lips always suggests something more than simple friendship," says one young man. And a woman echoes that sentiment with the conclusion that, "It's such an intimate act that I wouldn't feel comfortable kissing a friend."

Feel free to experiment with this kiss; it could lead to becoming better friends with someone. For example, one thirteen-year-old says, "I really want to make out with this guy I know kind of well. But I don't want to go out with him. How do I ask him, or do I?" The most honest way is to ask the guy up front: "Do you think it's possible to kiss and remain just friends?" In a roundabout way, this is suggesting that you want to kiss *him*. If he's not insulted, he'll probably be complimented, and your wish may come true.

But the flip side of the coin is reported by one attractive young woman who had many male admirers. "If I kiss a guy, I never hear from him again. It's a horrible problem for me. I guess guys think a kiss means a commitment. So if I'm just doing it for friendly reasons, they get insulted and never call me back." One way around this problem is to label a kiss as just a "friendly kiss" before you do it. But that adds the burden of talking about a kiss beforehand, almost always a sure way to spoil the fun and surprise of a kiss between friends.

What is a comet kiss?

Nothing is more romantic than the night sky when there's a comet or meteor shower on display. Every year thousands of lucky stargazers are rewarded with these spectacular fireworks. Kissing while a comet passes overhead is an event that will stay in your mind and heart forever. The trick to accomplishing a comet kiss is to predict when a comet or meteor shower will occur. There are many web sites that will guide you. These events aren't limited to amateur astronomers. Anyone can find out when the next appearance of periodic comets is scheduled to occur. Then you can hurry out with your lover, binoculars in hand, and enjoy one of the most romantic kisses ever.

CHAPTER SEVEN

Trendy Kisses

What is lip-o-suction?

Popular in Puerto Rico and some big cities on the East Coast, lip-o-suction (the first syllable is pronounced "lip") is a kiss for lovers who like to experiment. And all the experimentation takes place with the lips.

Jessica does it to Chucky whenever she gets the opportunity. It's her special way of saying she loves him—and wants to hold onto him! She begins by giving him a few regular kisses. Then she focuses on his lower lip, kissing and sucking it hard. Sometimes she has to remind herself not to bite into him like a ripe tomato. She actually has to restrain herself!

As she sucks his lower lip forcefully, Chucky begins kissing her upper lip. Because when she's kissing his lower lip, the only thing he *can* get hold of is her upper lip.

From this first position of the lip-o-suction kiss, Jessica likes to play with his lower lip. She has total control over it! And she loves that! She pulls it gently with her teeth—not intending to hurt him at all. Over and over she plays with his lip, tugging on it, pulling it out, then letting it snap back into place. *Zoing! Zo-*

ing! Zoing! How sensual it feels! And how bizarre! She's actually chewing on another person's lip! It's such a weird feeling, but a wickedly good one, too. She feels very connected with him whenever she does it.

And every time she bites into his lower lip and he allows it, she feels that she's in the driver's seat. It's a feeling she loves. It's like staking her claim to a man when she lip-o-suctions him.

Then they reverse!

When is the best time for lip-o-suction?

When you're tired of the same old french kisses, tired of simple lip kisses—that's the time for lip-o-suction. You may find the sensation powerful enough to reawaken your interest in each other's mouths just when you thought it was impossible. And don't feel silly doing it—the kiss is really catching on! Lip-o-suction is a trendy alternative to french kissing. I learned about it from a group of sixteen-year-olds from Puerto Rico. According to the kissing survey, the kiss is becoming more well known across the United States.

Are there really trends in kissing?

Absolutely. Like fashion, some kisses become popular for a while, then fade away into relative obscurity. Take the electric kiss, for example. Very popular in the 1930s and 40s, the kiss dropped almost totally out of sight in the 60s and 70s. Recently, with the invention of machines that can be hooked up to a battery to give you an added shock, the kiss has started to become more popular again. Similarly, lip-o-suction was described in the 2,000-year-old Indian love manual, the *Kama Sutra*. Then it fell out of favor. Today, with the advent of mass communication, television, and movies, kissing trends like lip-o-suction are enjoying a resurgence in popularity. Which is why it's a good idea to watch how people kiss in the movies—you can sometimes pick up a few pointers for your own kissing as long as you don't take their Hollywood technique too seriously.

What is a vacuum kiss?

This kiss is actually more popular than its unusual name might at first suggest. The vacuum kiss is done by sucking the air out of your partner's mouth and lungs during a kiss. It may sound a bit dangerous, but actually the kiss is quite safe when done with a moderate amount of force. And it can be a real blast to feel the vacuum run through your mouth and air pipe when your lover does it to you unexpectedly.

Because 60 percent of people have never experienced a vacuum kiss, it's a good one to try on an unsuspecting partner. One woman told me, "I'm so glad you wrote about this kiss, because my boyfriend was doing it to me, and I thought something was going terribly wrong." She felt like she was being turned inside out during his vacuum kisses. But that's just the sign of a great kiss and a great kisser. All the best kisses make you lose your head and cause a visceral reaction in sensitive souls, and this one is certainly no exception.

What are some variations in vacuum kissing?

The following variations will take you from easiest to most difficult—

❧ **Simple vacuum kiss.** The girl sucks air out of the boy's mouth. Anybody can do it.

- **Advanced vacuum.** She sucks air out of his mouth *and* lungs. This can be a big surprise if the guy doesn't expect it. It occurs accidentally to about 40 percent of lovers when, for example, the guy happens to be exhaling as the girl is inhaling. The guy will feel like he's a balloon being deflated.
- **Advanced vacuum II.** She sucks air out of his mouth while he allows air to be inhaled through his nose. Just a little trick you can try.
- **Double vacuum.** Keep your lips sealed tightly together as you both suck air out of each other's mouth. This makes the inside of your mouth feel like a bicycle tire.
- **Reverse vacuum.** The girl exhales directly into her boyfriend's mouth, and he simultaneously breathes in. It's an awesome feeling! Then they reverse. He exhales while she inhales his breath deep into her lungs. "It's a little scary and exciting at the same time," says a girl who's tried it. "It can make you dizzy." The fun part is that you'll be merging your life's breath, your air. It's an intense and intimate feeling!

During this kiss, carbon dioxide that was in your boyfriend's bloodstream is released into his lungs and travels out his mouth into your lungs and gets absorbed into your bloodstream. It is the most amazing physical fusion you can experience.

Do tongue piercings add to kissing pleasure?

Yes, according to almost all who have them. People who don't have them also report that it's exciting to kiss people who do. This is one of the trendiest things to impact the kissing scene today. Many young people are intrigued by the possibilities of having tongue barbell studs and they report that they're terrific fun while kissing because they increase the number of sensations that can be experienced during a kiss.

"I really want to get a tongue stud," says a nineteen-year-old college student who already has a navel ring. She's talking to her friend, who is equally interested in getting one. "I'd really like to know what it feels like."

A friend of theirs has one and tells them what it's like:

"My piercing in my mouth is called a barbell stud. It has a ball on top, with an attached post, and another ball on the other end that screws on and off for the removal of the jewelry.

"My boyfriend just got his tongue pierced too, and it definitely adds to the pleasure of kissing. I absolutely like it a lot better, because you can feel the ball on the end. You can also get a cover for the ball on the top of your tongue. It's called an atom. The cover is a hollow silicone bead that has a bunch of nubs and projections on it, so it slides right onto the ball. In other words, it's a French tickler. A good tip is to hold an ice cube in your mouth to get the piercing nice and cold, and then, YOWZERZ!!!!!!!!!!!!!!!!! Any area of the body, pierced or not, will definitely love it."

I personally would *not* recommend that you get a tongue piercing. But I do recommend kissing someone who's had it done. It is an indescribable experience.

What is the upside-down kiss?

You're sitting on the couch one evening when Brad comes into the room and stands behind you. Intrigued, you lean back and look up at him. He's glancing down at you. From this unusual angle, he doesn't even look like your boyfriend anymore. And you find that strangely exciting! It could be anybody—a total stranger!

Now he leans down toward you. Of course, you know it's him, but the mere thought that it's another guy makes your heart race! It's exciting! What does this guy have in mind? Why is he leaning over you like this? Maybe he likes you! Maybe he's so madly in love with you he wants to kiss you! What else could he be thinking! Of course he wants to kiss you! And that thought fires your imagination to a white hot intensity.

He's leaning down for a kiss!

Upside down!

Now his face gets closer, and you can feel the heat from his lips on yours. How strange he looks, all topsy-turvy! How strange and how amusing!

Your heart is straining now, straining as if it would burst. It wants to kiss. It wants the connection to happen, even if it's . . . upside down!

And then it does happen!

His lips touch yours. In this inverted position, it feels so disorienting. His full lower lip is pressed gently to your upper lip. Your lower lip is touching his upper lip. How confusing! How chaotic! How absolutely delicious and how forbidden! How really wrong it feels! How wrong . . . and how right!

The upside-down kiss is a kiss to try when your mind needs a flip-flop. It's a kiss that feels like a roller-coaster ride, a kiss that will turn your world upside down and inside out. It's a kiss that's so easy to do, most lovers never even remember to do it.

You've got to make special plans to do an upside-down kiss. Write yourself a note. Write it on your hand. In invisible ink. Upside down.

How can I become a trendy kisser?

There's just one trick to becoming a trendy kisser. You've got to discover the trends. And the best way to do this is to talk to your classmates and friends. As amazing as it may seem, most people don't discuss their kissing techniques with other people. They consider it private. But if you ask, you'll be surprised at how readily people seem to open up on this topic. You can pick up trendy new ideas about kissing techniques from the most unlikely people. You'll also stimulate your imagination. Next time you and your partner are together, all those discussions will come rushing back to your mind. Before you know it, you'll be doing trendy new kisses like lip-o-suction so regularly that you'll need to discover new trends and new kissing styles. (If you do, you're invited to email them to me for inclusion in the next edition of this book.)

What if my boyfriend kisses me in a trendy way that I don't like?

The first step is to get him to laugh at your reaction. So try to be funny. Say something like, "Whoa, partner! Hold your horses. Get off your ox. Slow down! Back up. Put on the emergency brake! Hold everything! Cease and desist." Then when he backs off, you have some time to think and breathe. Next, discuss the new kiss with him. Tell him you never had your tongue sucked before. Say it hurts. Say you can't breathe. Say you need some time to think about it. Say you want to consult a kissing specialist, a dentist, your minister—anything to give yourself some more time to think.

Another good strategy is to bring the subject up with him at a time when you're *not* kissing. Tell him something nice about his kissing style to make him relax. Then hit him with the bad news, "But honey you can never suck my tongue like that again. Because it reminds me of the time I almost drowned." Make something up if you need to. He'll believe it and, funny thing is, so will you. Remember, you have to fight for your right to be kissed the way you like. If you don't like the newest trend, don't do it. There are plenty of other kisses you *will* enjoy, so why spend time doing the ones you don't?

What is a combination kiss?

Not satisfied with one kiss at a time, some lovers combine techniques into mixes of two or more styles. Surprise and inventiveness are the key. A combination kiss might start with a lip kiss, change midstream into lip-o-suction, add a vacuum kiss, and wind up with the staple of all kissing, another lip kiss. The delightful combinations a young man can dream up on the spot are as endless as his imagination. His girlfriend will never tire of the variety, especially if he does them with feeling. The only thing he'll have to worry about is when she sighs and says, "Do that again, Harold!" How is he ever supposed to repeat that little combination—a biting spanking kiss that became an upside-down sliding eye kiss? He could hurt himself in the attempt . . .

CHAPTER EIGHT

Kissing Around the World

How do Eskimos kiss?

They don't kiss like the rest of us! In fact, numerous anthropologists have revealed that their kiss, popularly known as the Eskimo kiss, is more than a simple rubbing of the noses. It's a rather elaborate procedure that can be simulated like this—

- Face each other.
- Get so close that the tips of your noses touch.
- Run your nose along your partner's until it bumps into his or her face. Meanwhile the tip of your partner's nose should be hitting you in the face, too.
- Repeatedly flutter your eyelashes.
- Smack your lips—without kissing!
- Draw air in through your lips as you smack them.
- Keep smacking your lips, inhaling the delicious fragrance of your partner through your mouth!
- Now fight with your noses. Actually bat them back and forth! Don't be timid.

- Finally, press your nose into your partner's cheek—and hold it there!
- Keep your faces pressed together like that for at least thirty seconds. The Eskimos do it for even longer when it's cold out.

Why is the Eskimo kiss important?

Westerners sometimes have a slight case of xenophobia when it comes to foreign traditions, a fear of being perceived as different from everyone else. But studying the Eskimo kiss can help you in your own kissing; there are aspects of it that are totally appropriate and acceptable for Western kissers. In fact, some parts of the Eskimo kiss are almost required. For example, when kissing lip-to-lip, it's vitally important to know that your nose can slide along and rest on the side of your partner's nose, your heads slightly tilted and askew. Many people believe that they have to kiss head-on, straight as an arrow. This is just not the case, because your heads would be limited to the merest lip contact.

What other kissing tips can I learn from the Eskimos?

The Eskimo kiss is also helpful in showing Westerners how to break off from a kiss. Many young people are quite enthusiastic about kissing, but after they get into a kiss, they don't know how to get out! One of the easiest and funniest ways to terminate a kiss is with a little nose fight. You bump the tip of your nose into your partner's a few times and smile at him or her. That playful little fight is like a wave good-bye. Then you can break off with no hard feelings between the two of you.

Another technique the Eskimos have perfected is the face

press, in which you push your nose into your lover's cheek and hold it there for an extended period of time. Many Westerners are fond of this maneuver, and it's a wonderful way to stay close and connected without having to kiss lip-to-lip. Frank Sinatra was a big fan of the face press, but he did a variation of it where he just pressed his cheek to the woman's cheek, which allowed him to show affection for his partner but also get his full face into the picture if a publicity photographer was around. You can also use the face press whenever you need to take a short break from kissing but don't want to move far from your loved one.

What is the Japanese kiss?

It's a kiss for shy people, because in Asia people are very bashful about kissing. In fact one Japanese-American woman says, "If my mother ever sees people kissing on television, she shuts the set right off." This shyness pervades Japan, China, Taiwan, and even Korea. Public kissing is very rare in these countries. Lovers have to be quite circumspect in their kissing practices. The Japanese kiss was developed specifically for Westerners, the directions gleaned from actual observations of how people kiss in Asia. Now you, too, can enjoy the delicate pleasures of the Japanese kiss.

- Stand at attention. Keep your hands at your sides!
- Your boyfriend or girlfriend should do the same.
- Glance left and right to make sure no one's watching.
- Lean toward your partner.
- Keep your mouth closed!
- Lean closer, bending at the waist until your lips touch briefly.
- Do not open your mouth or rub your mouths together. Sim-

ply touch your closed lips to your partner's for a fraction of a second.

➤ Immediately stand back at attention.

➤ Look left and right to make sure no one saw anything.

"What good is this nonsense?" you ask. "It's too childish for me."

Ah, my dear bourgeois imperialist culture-bound stick-in-the-mud friend! The way of the child is the way of wisdom. Sometimes kissing can become too adult, too advanced, too complex. Take a giant step back from all that complexity. Open your mind. Embrace the ancient Taoist way. Less is more.

Are Europeans better kissers?

The nearly universal consensus from people who have kissed them suggests that they are. And even if they aren't better, they're at least different in some significant and interesting ways. The primary difference is in intimacy, but there are some other things that people around the world can learn from Europeans about kissing.

Like what?

Well, for one thing, Europeans don't generally view kissing as merely a prelude to sex. Instead they kiss for the sake of kissing, which allows them to get into the kissing experience in a more enthusiastic and wholehearted way. Women who have kissed both American and European men are quite certain that their experiences kissing Europeans were more memorable for just this reason. "He kissed me like that was *all* he wanted to do, and I loved it," says one young woman.

What other tricks do Europeans use?

Although the french kiss has nothing to do with France (see page 38), apparently Europeans are better at tongue kisses, too. "They don't choke you with their tongue like some American boys," says a college student. They use their tongue with variety and subtle moves that communicate wordlessly with their partner.

"The way he used to play chase with my tongue and his tongue made me want it to never stop," says another woman.

Europeans are also known for talking with their hands. And when it comes to kissing, they use their hands much more skillfully than people on other continents. Most North Americans are puzzled about what to do with their hands while kissing. Europeans gently caress their partners—they don't grope! And they aren't distracted by the fact that their lips are in contact. Like a piano player, they keep both hands moving, running them up and down their partner's back, playing with their lover's hair, squeezing their partner's waist and caressing their body.

How can I kiss like a European?

If you really want to excite your partner, try these things that Europeans do—

- ❧ Give greeting kisses to your partner. Europeans do this to friends. But you should do it to your lover. And make sure those greeting kisses are on the lips.
- ❧ Kiss a number of times when saying good-bye.
- ❧ Press your body into your lover when kissing. It's a good way to be close.
- ❧ Kiss just for the sake of kissing.
- ❧ And kiss more often in public.

Are there any bizarre kissing customs around the world?

Yes. In the South Pacific, natives on a group of islands known as the Trobriand Islands would think we were crazy for talking about kissing the way we have in this book. Because they don't kiss like us at all. Their kissing practices were described in 1929 by Bronislaw Malinowski in a book called *The Sexual Life of Savages*. Be forewarned: blood is sometimes involved in this kiss. And when we demonstrate it in front of college students, people in the audience often faint. So we always have a medic on hand. To date, three college students have had to be taken out on stretchers as a result of fainting when they saw this kiss.

What on earth is a Trobriand Islands kiss?

In the South Pacific, a group of people live on the beautiful Trobriand Islands. Their islands are full of tropical foods and tall green vegetation. Because their climate is so wonderful they live in grass huts. And they are much more open about showing affection than we are in the United States. When they are nine and ten years old, they begin going into the big grass huts and playing kissing games. Two or three couples can use one grass hut at a time. It's like a communal living and partying space. They usually kiss in a squatting position on a grass mat. They hug and caress each other. And they rub their tongues together and *suck* on each other's tongues.

As their kissing becomes more intense, they begin to suck and bite on each other's lower lip so vigorously that it often bleeds. At the height of their passion, they bite each other's chins and then they begin to nibble at their partner's eyelashes.

(Which is why it's a status symbol in the Trobriand Islands to have short eyelashes—it proves you're popular with the opposite sex.)

This is an actual kiss that is popular in the South Pacific. But I suggest you discuss it with your partner before trying it.

CHAPTER NINE

The Emotional Side
of Kissing

What are emotional kissing problems?

When you kiss you should feel so good that you think you're going to explode with pleasure. You should feel like the top of your head is coming off or like your heart is racing so fast you're going to die. Any psychological condition that prevents you from trembling, sweating, laughing uncontrollably or getting dizzy, anything that prevents you from feeling pins and needles throughout your body, anything that prevents your heart from racing at a frighteningly fast but excitingly pleasant pace—in short, anything that prevents you from fully enjoying all the pleasures of kissing is an emotional kissing problem. Please note: none of these reactions is the problem . . . instead it is the *absence* of these sensations of euphoria that is the problem. And almost everyone suffers from such problems to one degree or another at some point in his or her life. Emotional problems encompass all the mental roadblocks to kissing enjoyment that you may experience, such as kissing phobias, shyness, uncertainty, and the overbearing presence of parents.

What role do parents play in common kissing problems?

Parents are often your biggest emotional problem when it comes to kissing pleasure. I can't tell you how many young people say, "My parents won't let me have your kissing books in the house." Any parent who won't let his or her kids read this type of book is making a tragic mistake. In addition, young people routinely tell me things like, "My mother doesn't allow me to kiss my boyfriend." One girl said, "My mom follows me and spies on me to make sure I don't kiss boys." This kind of parental misbehavior will only encourage kids to devise ways to outwit their fuddy-duddy caretakers. *Note to parents:* Lighten up on your kids. (And you might try more kissing yourselves!)

What is the biggest emotional kissing problem?

The inability to understand what your partner is thinking and feeling is the number-one emotional kissing problem. Almost everyone has felt the effects of this problem to some extent, wondering what their boyfriend or girlfriend is thinking while kissing. When your uncertainty about the other person interferes with your own kissing enjoyment, it rises to the level of an emotional kissing problem. Many young people ask, "How can I get over my fear of not pleasing my partner when I kiss?" If you could read their mind, then you'd immediately see what they want when kissing, and you could devote yourself to pleasing them. But since that's impossible, you'll have to rely on what they communicate to you—both verbally and otherwise—about what they're looking for in a kiss.

What is kissing phobia?

Your heart races, your knees shake, your palms sweat—it feels exactly like the euphoria you're supposed to experience when kissing . . . only you're *not* kissing at all, you're just standing there with your girlfriend, and you feel frozen and paralyzed. This is a more common problem than you may think, with approximately 15 percent of lovers reporting that they suffer from some fear of kissing. The fear usually doesn't lead to a complete avoidance of kissing; instead, its clearest manifestation is in young people who admit that they don't let themselves go completely while kissing. For example: "I'm fifteen years old, and every time I kiss my girlfriend I, in a way, pull back. I don't know why. I know I love her. What's wrong with me?" This condition stems from fear of pleasure, and it's especially common in people who are very conscientious and driven to do well. Type A people sometimes have to learn to relax into a kissing session. Put on some music or go outside into a park where you can find a secluded spot. Then relax and keep in mind that you don't have to do everything perfectly when kissing. Sometimes it even helps to try and purposely make some mistakes!

What if I'm shy?

Believe it or not, shy people are the most fun people to kiss, so don't worry excessively about being shy. In fact, it may turn out to be an asset, drawing extroverted people toward you. You're a challenge for them, and you're special for that reason. If your parents are also shy, you may have inherited the disposition from them, in which case, therapy can sometimes help. Or you can tackle your kissing shyness by talking about kissing with friends and studying how actors kiss in movies. The more you expose yourself to kissing, the more likely you are to overcome your shyness. In your own life, work up to kissing sessions slowly. Try starting with a hand kiss or a good-night kiss. These icebreakers will help you gain confidence. When you see that your partner responds positively to your attention, you'll gradually become more courageous.

My boyfriend told me my tongue was too short. What should I do?

An attractive young woman said this after a recent lecture in Ohio. She added: "Ever since then I've had a complex about it." I told her to stick her tongue out. Her tongue reached all the way down to her chin! I pointed out that her tongue was not short; if anything, it was longer than average. Many young lovers get complexes because of an immature comment a partner makes. The best thing to do, I told her, is to realize that it doesn't matter how long your tongue is. You can kiss just fine with a long or short tongue. You don't have to insert your tongue very far into your partner's mouth for a french kiss, for example. Sometimes just a tiny bit is enough. If someone makes an immature remark to you about your kissing style or ability, ignore it. It just shows his or her own ignorance.

I'm afraid my boyfriend won't like the way I kiss. What can I do?

First, kissing is partly a natural phenomenon. There's no right or wrong way to kiss. Keep that firmly in mind! No boyfriend should ever tell you that you "don't know how to kiss."

There are, however, some things that can be learned about kissing. You can learn *how* someone else likes to be kissed. One great way to do that is to tell your boyfriend that you're not going to kiss him back for three full minutes. You want him to kiss you the way *he* likes. While he kisses you, take note of his kissing style to see what he likes. Does he give gentle kisses or does he press forcefully against you with his lips? Does he use his tongue? Does he give short little kisses or long, deep ones?

Afterward you can reverse roles and tell him not to kiss you back while you kiss him the way *you* like to be kissed. In this way, you'll learn about each other's preferences.

Another thing that can be learned is gentleness. Watch some romantic movies and study how the actors kiss. You can actually pick up ideas from some of them. You can also learn from kissing your own hand. I know it sounds silly, but you can feel the kiss on your hands and lips, and you'll get a sense of how your kiss feels to someone else.

If you're in college, you can also ask your roommates how they kiss. They'll probably be flattered to tell you. Better yet, ask them to show you by kissing a picture of a man in a magazine. (You could also try this. Get an issue of GQ and kiss the models in the magazine yourself. Again, it may sound silly, but you'll learn from doing it.) Another idea is to ask a boy (you'll have to carefully select a guy who's only a platonic friend, and explain your question to him). Reread the section on the friendly kiss (page 101–3) for pointers. Any guy would be flattered to show a young woman how to kiss.

Should you kiss to make up?

Yes. Because a make-up kiss is a convenient way to symbolically indicate that things are fixed up after an argument. As one woman says, "a make-up kiss is the best way to become reconciled, and if the argument isn't resolved, the attempted make-up kiss will let you know." To help it work, do it with sincerity. And precede it with a little phrase such as, "Let's never fight again!" or "I was right after all."

How can I deal with kissing rejection?

This question is for people who say, "If, after kissing someone, they tell you that they wanted a more platonic relationship and hadn't know you 'felt that way,' how does one recover?" The answer is that you should try to find someone else who'll give you more respect and affection. That should be rather easy, since this person is giving you virtually none. Second, try to maintain a relationship with the first person to see if their feelings might change. By the time you find someone new, the first person may fall in love with you. In that case, refer to my advice on how to kiss two people at once (page 148). By the way, having two people in love with you simultaneously does not qualify as a problem.

How can I overcome extreme nervousness?

Next time your boyfriend wants to kiss you, admit that you're too nervous for real kisses, and suggest that he start slowly and easily by just kissing your *hand*. I am 100 percent serious. Make a little mouth with your thumb and first finger, and tell him to kiss that while you pretend it's your mouth. For the first hour you're together he's not allowed to kiss your real mouth, just your hand, wrist, and arm (no higher than the shoulder). This will work, because it will prove to you that you can be *kissed* and remain calm. After you try this for one date, you can progress.

The next time you get together, the rule will be that he can only kiss you on the cheek, not on the mouth, for the entire duration of that date. Then on your next date, he'll be allowed to kiss your mouth . . . but no tongue. Taking it step-by-step is guaranteed to calm you down, and it will be exciting for him, too. You'll be perfectly relaxed because you'll know exactly how far things are going each day. This technique is based on a sound psychological principle: if you get too nervous, regress to something simpler which you can do with ease. Only progress further when you feel comfortable with it.

How can I get him to kiss the way he did when we first met?

Unfortunately, you can't. You're going to have to accept the fact that not only isn't he kissing you that old magical way, but you're not interacting with him the way you did when you first met. Then everything was new, different, magical. The excitement of the unknown is one of the keys to kissing pleasure. Probably the closest you can come to recapturing those early romantic feelings will be to go to new places and try different types of kisses.

How can I bring back the excitement of our first kiss?

The bad news is that it's usually impossible to bring back the excitement of your first kiss, because that kiss is a magic moment, never to be duplicated. So, just try to enjoy the good feeling of being together. That calmness you feel in a long-term relationship is a sign of mature love. After a number of years, the excitement does wear off. Then true love begins, which is a more tranquil experience than the feeling you get at the outset of a relationship. Many people go from person to person seeking that initial romantic excitement. It's like the feeling you get when you eat chocolate—a kind of love high.

If you really need romantic excitement, try pretending your lover is someone else. Get your partner a disguise, different clothes, even a mask if necessary. Or just fantasize. Marilyn Monroe routinely did this when kissing on camera. Just be careful not to let your lover realize what you're doing.

Why does kissing become *less* intense in long-term relationships?

When people get used to their partners, some of the excitement wears off. This is normal, and it happens to everyone. But it's not always easy to accept the fact that part of the romance will fade away. If you want to add some sparks back into your kissing encounters, try a few of the different kisses in this book.

Are men more likely to tire of kissing?

Yes. Women outnumber men four to one in saying that they want more kissing in their relationships. If your partner gets tired of kissing sooner than you, try new kissing techniques such as the teasing kiss, the vacuum kiss, lip-o-suction, and other unusual kisses (all described in this book). Surprise kisses and public kisses can also heat up an otherwise sluggish kissing session between longtime lovers.

How can I tell whether he's emotionally into kissing me or whether he's just enjoying me physically?

One way to tell is if he seems interested in you when you talk about things in general. Try comparing him with your friends and family or a trusted teacher. Notice how they listen to you and care about you and your issues. Does he listen to you the same way? Does he share your interests? Does he care about you in the same way? You really cannot tell during the kiss itself; you have to make this determination prior to, or after, the kiss.

What is my girlfriend *really* looking for in my kisses?

She probably wants you to *go slow.* Women usually take longer to heat up than guys. So going too fast may send her the wrong message. For you, the message may be, "Honey, I love you! I'm crazy about you," whereas for her, the message she's getting is, "He just cares about what's happening physically." A pretty twenty-year-old blonde says, "I don't trust guys. All they seem to want is sex. It's hard to find someone who likes me for me. It's hard to find someone nice in college."

Guys, slow down. Gals will love you. How can you do it? Here's a hint. Try to let them make the first move. In other words, kiss, but don't go too fast. Don't escalate the contact or the level of intimacy. For example, let them french-kiss you first.

I'm a better kisser than my boyfriend—how can I teach him without hurting his feelings?

If your partner is a less-experienced kisser, help him learn. Show him some new kissing techniques. To make it easier on his ego, you might want to ask him to show you how he likes being kissed. Then show him how you like being kissed. It will seem like an equal game to him, but actually you'll be teaching him a lot more. Before long he'll be giving just as good as he gets.

What if a guy tries to kiss me and I don't want him to?

The classiest response is to simply give him some funny excuse that will put an end to it immediately. Anything you can think of, such as—

- Sorry, I don't kiss until the *second* date.
- My parents don't allow me to kiss.
- I have a cold.
- Let's not and say we did.

CHAPTER TEN

The Technical Side of Kissing

What if my boyfriend laughs while kissing me?

Relax. This does *not* mean you're doing anything wrong. Just the opposite! Laughing while kissing is a sign of intense pleasure. More than 90 percent of people occasionally laugh while kissing. You should never be insulted if your partner laughs or giggles when kissing. It's actually an indication that you're doing things right! In fact, you should be worried if he *never* laughs. If that's the case, memorize a few kissing jokes that you can spring on him while kissing to loosen him up. You can always murmur something like, "You have such nice nostrils" in the middle of a kiss. This usually gets a laugh . . . unless he actually thinks he has terrific nostrils.

What if my girlfriend starts to cry?

Kiss her on the eyes. This is the most romantic and gentle response. It acknowledges how she feels, accepts her tears completely, and shows what a caring guy you are. About 2 percent of people cry when kissing, either out of sadness or out of joy.

I'm really clumsy, and when I try to kiss someone, I wind up tripping or losing my balance. Any suggestions?

There are four things you can try in a situation like this. First, kiss while sitting down. Second, try to get her backed up against a wall, which can provide some stability for you. Third, put your hands on her shoulders for balance. And fourth, try to wait a little more before you start kissing. In other words, maybe she'll make the first move . . . then she'll be the one who trips and loses her balance.

How can I knock her socks off with a kiss?

The surest advice I can give guys about how to excite a woman with a kiss is to suggest that you kiss her neck and ears. One of the most surprising things the kissing survey revealed was that of all the places women like to be kissed, their favorite spot, aside from the mouth, is the neck. That's right—the neck. If you're dating a woman and you've never kissed her neck, have you got a surprise in store for you!

Now, you may ignore this advice just because neck kisses aren't a super turn-on for you (only about 10 percent of guys say they get excited by neck kisses). But there is a clear gender-based difference at work here. Just recently I got email from a fifteen-year-old girl who says, "I love it when guys kiss my neck. It sends chills up and down my entire body. Another place I love to be kissed is on the earlobe." (See also pages 65–69.)

The other advice is something that most men routinely overlook, so if you take note of this you'll have a sharp advantage over these guys. And that is to *be gentle*. Listen to this remark from a twenty-one-year-old. "Why is it that most guys think when they kiss a girl, they have to clean her tonsils during the process? They don't understand that when you're kissing a girl, the best part is the slow, passionate kisses that mean so much more. Anyone can stick their tongue in your mouth, but it takes patience to make the kiss 100 percent better. It tells a girl that you care and want to enjoy that very moment with her."

That, my friend, is advice worth remembering. Can you believe it? Ironically, when it comes to women, gentleness will probably blow her socks off a lot faster than a french kiss.

How can I stop my boyfriend from sucking my face off?

Unfortunately, some people have a tendency to suck vigorously during a kiss. This is a matter of personal taste and style, but you may find it annoying. The best solution is to talk to him about it when you're not kissing. Don't try to discuss it while you're being intimate because your emotions may be too involved. But when you're both relaxed and in a friendly mood, ask him how he likes being kissed. Then tell him you like nice, gentle kisses. Explain that you're a lover, not a lollipop. If this doesn't work, try sucking on *his* ear and nose and see how he likes it. If all else fails, tell him you're going to give him an elbow in the rib cage every time he kisses you in a way you don't like. I guarantee this will put a stop to his infantile behavior right away. Which isn't to say that kissing shouldn't be infantile. It certainly should be, and that's half the fun of it. But enough is enough, isn't it? In love, as in war, you have to know where to draw the line.

Should I keep my eyes closed?

This is optional. But about 66 percent of people do. Most of the people who like to keep their eyes closed say it helps them concentrate on the feelings of the kiss. On the other hand, one out of three people likes to look. One young man says, "I like to see where I'm aiming with a kiss and where my lips will hit." A young woman says she likes to look over her boyfriend's shoulder into a mirror to experience simultaneously the physical pleasure of the kiss and the visual picture of them standing together. Don't be insulted if your boyfriend likes to keep his eyes open when kissing. Indeed, you should be flattered. It means he finds you attractive.

This question is the one that actually got me started writing about kissing in the first place. A date once told me I should keep my eyes closed when kissing, and not believing this, I went to the library to try and find some information to back up my belief that you could keep your eyes open. Discovering virtually nothing written on the subject, I decided to write *The Art of Kissing* to provide answers to the questions I myself had. I was very pleased to find that about 33 percent of people agree with me and look when kissing.

Can you change a guy's kissing style without actually telling him?

No. With one exception. Giving my book as a gift has been known to work miracles. But without telling him, he'll never know because he can't read your mind. You could try going to a romantic movie and commenting on the kissing and saying what you like about it, but that's a long shot. You've usually got to communicate with words before you can communicate in a compatible way with kisses.

How can I keep from throwing up when a guy sticks his tongue down my throat?

First of all, no guy should be giving you this much tongue, so don't feel bad about fighting back. If you don't want to bite his tongue, you can take the easier route and tell him to stop it or you'll stick your finger up his nose. If this doesn't stop him, I'd actually stick my finger up his nose or in his ear—not to be rude or anything—but to good-naturedly get him to pay attention.

Why couldn't my boyfriend breathe while kissing?

This is a common complaint, especially with people who have just started kissing romantically. Most people have to learn how to breathe through their noses during a kiss. Or they can try taking breaks to breathe through their mouth. Your boyfriend probably just needs more practice. It's kind of like scuba diving or snorkeling. In fact, snorkeling is good practice for kissing.

How can I relax my lips?

Some people tense up during kissing and as a result their lips have a harsh and puckered feel. For example, one young woman says, "My last boyfriend was my first french kiss, and he said it was good but that I needed to relax my lips more. What did he mean by this? I'm afraid that I'll have Jell-O lips next time!" He probably meant that your lips were too puckered up. But he would have been wrong if he suggested that you keep your lips relaxed all through a french kiss. That's like trying to eat an apple after getting a shot of novocaine—you won't know what you're doing and will feel out of control. Instead, just remember to vary the pressure of your lips, sometimes tense and puckered, sometimes relaxed. The same for your tongue. Take an active part in the kiss, and you'll be fine. In other words, relax and enjoy it.

Is there anything risky about kissing?

Since french kissing involves the exchange of saliva, it can lead to the transmission of colds or viruses like the flu, herpes, or mononucleosis. However, although there will be about 70 million AIDS cases worldwide by the year 2000, there is only one recorded case of AIDS transmission via kissing, a rare and unique case that involved blood transfer through cuts in both the man's and woman's mouths. To date no case of AIDS reported to the Centers for Disease Control and Prevention has been attributed to exposure to saliva alone. So there is no question that kissing is one of the safest romantic things two people can do together.

What is a hickey?

A hickey is a reddish mark on the skin caused by kissing, biting, or sucking. In previous generations, people went to great lengths to conceal their hickeys, with makeup, scarves, and turtlenecks. Today, however, they're something of a prized fashion statement. Many young people love getting hickeys because they believe it shows they're popular with the opposite sex.

How can I give my girlfriend a hickey?

There are three ways to do this. The first is to simply kiss her so vigorously that her skin eventually turns reddish in the spot you kissed. The second way is to bite her—*gently, please!*—while kissing. A little love nip on the back of her neck, for example, or on her shoulder, will typically leave a red mark. The third way is to suck your girlfriend's flesh during a kissing session. If you suck her arm, say, it will develop a red spot indicating capillary injury just below the surface of the skin. (In fact, you can do this to your own arm, just to see what a hickey looks like.) It may take a few minutes for the mark to appear. Sometimes it will take as long as half an hour to appear. That red or bluish spot is a hickey. And when she sees what you've done to her, depending on her frame of mind, she'll either love you or hate you! You can't always predict.

How do people attempt to get rid of hickeys?

Some silly suggestions from readers of my web page include: brush it with a toothbrush, press a cold spoon onto it, take a pencil eraser and put it in the center of the hickey and twirl it around, or pour vinegar on it.

Do any of these methods work?

No. None of these methods actually works. A hickey is a bruise. You can't get rid of a bruise by using a toothbrush or a cold spoon or a pencil eraser or vinegar. They're all folk cures that have absolutely no effectiveness whatsoever. Most of them will actually make the hickey worse. There is no way to get rid of a hickey except to give it time to heal by itself, like any other bruise. In the meantime, if you want to conceal a hickey, I suggest the age-old methods of using makeup, clothing, or a Band-Aid.

Is it okay to kiss with gum in my mouth? And what's the best way to do this?

Kissing with gum in your mouth is one of the most sensual things you can do. First of all, make sure you stop chewing on it when your boyfriend's tongue comes into your mouth or you're liable to chomp on his tongue. That's the most important thing. Chew when his tongue is out of your mouth, and remember to chew more gently and slowly than normal, just in case. Also be careful not to let it fall out into your hair, which can ruin your whole day, not to mention your romantic interlude. He can be kissing your lips while you chew. If you try this you'll feel like you're chewing him, when actually you're just chewing your gum. People who've done it say it feels like a mystical communion, almost as if you're devouring him. You have to concentrate more on the chewing at first, and let him carry the burden of kissing your outer lips. Then as you relax into the experience, you can chew while focusing on the feeling of the kiss, and you can pucker up a little while chewing and kind of kiss him back. Once he starts giving you some tongue, your gum should be placed to the side of your mouth so you can french-kiss. If you're not careful, he may steal your gum—try to prevent this by hiding the gum under your tongue. You may have to fight him off with your tongue if he's the kind of guy who would steal your gum. A gentleman chews his own gum when kissing a girl who's chewing too.

How can I tell if excessive wetness is my fault?

You can tell if it's your fault by swallowing during the kiss. If that cures the problem, you know you were the cause. If your kisses are still too wet, tell your lover to start swallowing. Appeal to his sense of fairness. Put it to him this way: "You've got to learn to take responsibility for your own saliva."

How do I kiss without dribbling everywhere?

Whenever you feel that you're getting too watery in the mouth, back off, bring your lips together, and give your partner a distracting little lip kiss on her upper or lower lip while you unobtrusively swallow. As silly as it may sound, you've got to swallow your own saliva. This may take some practice, but it's the best way to keep your kisses neat. About 25 percent of people complain about a lover's kisses being too wet. As you become more excited, however, your tolerance for wet kisses will increase and you may actually find wetter kisses more exciting. But for initial kisses, swallowing your own saliva is the easiest way to keep them relatively dry. You can do this while your mouths are in contact. You can also take a break, move your head back, and swallow. Or you can move down to the neck, kiss there, and swallow or even take a drink of water. Drinking something will actually clear your mouth for a neater, drier kiss. Another suggestion is to wipe your mouth and lips with a tissue or handkerchief. Finally, shorter kisses tend to be drier. So if you're worried about wet kisses, try cutting down the amount of time your kisses last.

How can I tactfully tell my boyfriend to stop drooling on me?

Tell him you heard about a little kissing game the two of you can play. It's called "Show Me How You Like to Be Kissed." You tell your lover boy that he can't kiss you for the next three minutes. He must keep his lips shut and not kiss you back at all. He's got to take it while you dish it out. Then show him by kissing him exactly how you like to be kissed. Kiss his neck if you like neck kisses. Kiss him with dry lips, anything you like. Then it's his turn. He's supposed to show you how he likes to be kissed while you just take it. He may learn a few things from this about how you like to kiss.

Also, rent the movie *Husbands* and watch it with him. It has a scene in which Peter Falk gets kissed for an entire minute by an Asian woman. She slobbers all over him at the end of the kiss. While watching it, casually say to your lover boy, "I would just hate to be kissed like that! I like nice dry kisses."

If all this subtlety fails, play another game, called "Honesty." It involves telling your partner something you like about them, followed by something you don't like. You can drop your hint during this game.

How can I tell my partner how I feel about him while kissing?

It's best to "say" it with your lips! If you do talk, keep it light and carefree. Say silly little romantic things, sweet nothings—"You have such nice eyelashes." Try to make him laugh. You can occasionally get serious, but don't overdo it. Keep it light, but make it sound romantic.

One young woman got worried when her boyfriend asked her what she was thinking while kissing, because she was thinking something random and irrelevant and didn't know whether to admit this to him. Never admit you're thinking about something trivial. This will hurt his feelings. Instead, say you're thinking about what kind of kiss you're going to give next, anything to fool him into thinking you're thinking about him. And then actually try to think about him for a few minutes.

Why do our teeth hit together?

Many people bump their teeth into their partner's when kissing because they're pressing too forcefully. Says one young woman, "When I kiss my boyfriend, our teeth quite often hit each other. It doesn't hurt, but it gets a bit embarrassing and sometimes we both start laughing. How do we stop this, or can we stop it at all?" One technique is to kiss less intensely. Try simpler lip kisses— avoid french kisses for a while. Then kiss the side of his mouth, the side of his lips, then his cheek, neck, ears, and tell him you like the same. Once you back off like this you may find that the problem stops. People with an overbite experience the problem more than others, but the only real solution is less forceful pressure while kissing or kissing at a less aggressive angle.

Will women be turned off by a large lower lip?

Quite the contrary—many women find a naturally large lower lip sensual. Plus, it should make it easy for you to kiss a woman's lower lip, since your lower lip can brush against the underside of her lower lip. But you should also be able to kiss her upper lip without difficulty. In this position, she'll be able to kiss and suck on your lower lip, which she may enjoy immensely. See how she reacts to it; you may find you have a romantic advantage having such a lip. If you notice women staring at your mouth, it's often a sign that they're daydreaming about kissing you. (And you thought they were just spacing out!)

Should I worry about having braces?

No—you should rejoice! Unfortunately, a lot of people feel self-conscious about having braces and kissing, but this is totally unjustified. In fact, having braces today is considered sexy by a growing number of young people. And here's why. First of all, braces are a sign of youth; most people with them are young. Second, braces draw attention to your mouth and your smile, making you appear cuter. Third, and most interestingly, with the trend today toward more body piercing and body jewelry, including tongue piercing, braces and retainers are moving into the realm of mouth jewelry. When you talk or smile, people who see you wearing braces are going to start viewing them as an *in* thing, especially if you get the metal kind that reflect light. And because it's exciting to kiss someone with braces, you may find yourself becoming more popular with the opposite sex.

If both people have braces, can they get stuck while kissing?

Yes. Braces do have hooks and wires that potentially can be a problem when kissing. However the problem is not serious as long as you follow the same path that you took to get stuck, *in reverse*. The areas where you can get stuck are limited, and dentists have assured me that if you're careful there should be no problem at all. Getting stuck happens very rarely, and the two people can always get unstuck again. They may actually enjoy the process and treat it like a game! So never let the fact that you have braces prevent you from kissing. (They just may provide a way to make you and your lover inseparable!)

How can I get my husband to brush his teeth more often?

Say these words to him at a time when you're not kissing: "Honey, I think I have bad breath. So I read up on it and found out how to cure it. There are a few things I can do, and I'm going to do them all—

❥ "Brush my teeth.
❥ "Use dental floss after every meal.
❥ "Brush my tongue. Yes, my tongue. You heard me right. I found out that brushing my tongue will remove bacteria and make my breath fresher. So I'll just use my toothbrush on my own tongue. It might feel funny, but who cares as long as it works!
❥ "Use mouthwash now and then.
❥ "Avoid eating onions and garlic on the day before I kiss you."

In other words, act like *you* have bad breath. He'll feel so sorry for you, he'll start doing the same thing. If he doesn't get the hint, don't kiss him. The way to avoid kissing him is to say: "I feel like I have bad breath and don't want to kiss." If he insists that your breath is fine, just tell him you don't think it is. Tell him you want to brush your teeth, and encourage him to do the same—then you'll kiss him.

How can I let a guy know I want to be kissed?

When you're on a date, do whatever you can to make eye contact and conversation. Then figure out some way to get closer to him. Sit next to him or stand close. Keep looking at him until you start to feel a magnetic attraction between you. Then at the right moment, step even closer to him, so close that you can feel the heat from his body. If necessary, think up some excuse for this: straighten his tie, ask him to look in your eye to see if there's something in it, or use some other excuse. Flirt with him, and he should get the message. This closeness is a strong signal that you're flirting and want to be kissed. If he's too dense to take the hint, you may have to be more direct, for example, by saying something like, "Oh, I feel dizzy. I think I need a kiss to wake me up." Sounds ridiculous, I know, but some guys need to be hit over the head with the message or they'll never act.

What should I do with my hands?

Run them up and down your partner's back. Try gently tugging on his hair. If you're short on cash, reach into his pockets and see if you can find any bills. I'm just kidding about looking for money, but putting your hands into your lover's pockets can really be fun. Just don't grope! The list of preferred activities includes—

- Run your hands up and down her back.
- Cup his face gently and softly.
- Hold her chin and steer it in the direction you need to kiss her.
- Grab his ears and turn his head whichever way suits you.
- Hug him tightly toward you, then release so he can breathe again.
- Hold her by the shoulders.
- Insert your thumbs under her arms.
- Stick your fingers in his hair.

- Hang your arms around his neck.
- Hold hands.

Can I talk while kissing?

Yes, and your partner will appreciate hearing from you, as long as you keep your comments light and fun. In fact, people who don't talk at least occasionally while kissing appear to be distant and uninterested. The key to talking and kissing is to talk directly into your partner's mouth and say something romantic. Occasionally you can break off from a kiss and whisper something silly and sweet in your partner's ear.

How should I touch my partner's hair when kissing?

Both men and women like you to play with their hair. Sometimes you can even pull your partner's hair, but don't treat it like a door chime. A gentle, loving stroke (and even a tug) usually does the trick.

When is the best time to change from one kiss to another?

Make your transitions from one kiss to another when you or your partner gets tired with the kiss you're currently doing. If you notice your lover getting a bored look on his face, one that says, "Hey, it's time for my nap!"—then do something new, like moving from a french kiss to a neck kiss. Another good time to make a transition to something different is when your partner is have a really good time. It's a subtle trick. You leave him just when the going gets good. This way he'll want you back again; he'll unconsciously be hungry for you and that great kiss.

CHAPTER ELEVEN

Kissing Secrets You Can Try Tonight

Is it fun to kiss in a car?

If you live in the United States and don't regularly kiss in a car, you're missing one of the greatest romantic thrills of your young life. After all, you've grown up in a society where cars symbolize status, fun, and romance. Cars often figure in romantic movies and are associated with stopping in a secluded spot and kissing. Don't be shy about following the crowd on this one; after all, the trend was created to give you romantic opportunities . . . so you might as well take advantage of them. Almost all men and women say they enjoy kissing in a car at least sometimes. "It's nice to know we're being watched when we kiss in his Mustang," says one young woman. "And there's no denying that I do get a kick out of being seen." (Those of you who live in urban areas and don't own cars can indulge in a little taxicab kissing. If you keep it discreet, it can be very romantic. If you park and kiss in a cab in New York City, for example, you're paying at a rate of about twenty-five cents per kiss, which is actually a pretty good deal . . .)

How can I improve my car kisses?

Begin by imagining you're in a movie. Instantly you'll become more aware of the lighting and the scene outside the car. For example, if it's nighttime, enjoy the reflections of the lights in your windshield and the crazy shadows that dance over you and your lover as you kiss. Most important, keep the car stereo on. If you need inspiration, rent romantic movies featuring cars, like *American Graffiti* or *Rebel Without a Cause*. Your friends can supply the names of plenty more.

Keep in mind, however, that you should wait until you're parked to kiss. There's a great scene in Albert Brooks's movie *Modern Romance* where he tries to kiss his girlfriend in a car while he's driving, and she cautions him to watch the road. He gives her a disappointed look and says, "A kiss is more important than life, isn't it?" That's such a sweet line . . . but play it safe; wait for the car to stop.

What's the best way to kiss at the movies?

In America, there are two places where it's almost mandatory to kiss while growing up: in cars and, of course, in movie theaters. The combination of the two, the drive-in theater, is equivalent to the superhighway of romance. Kiss in a drive-in and not only are you in a car, but people can see you and you're in a theater as well, hopefully watching a romantic film. So much romantic activity goes on there, they should rename them kiss-ins. Unfortunately, with the advent of multiscreen theaters in malls, the old drive-ins are a dying species.

In a theater, the best place to sit is in back where you won't bother the people who are trying to watch the movie. About 25 percent of moviegoers enjoy smooching during a show, at least some of the time. If you're one of them, there's a great game you can play called copy cat. The rules are simple: you kiss whenever the actors do. Other good times to kiss are when emotional scenes occur, such as when families come together or when people cry. Copy cat works best at romantic movies, but you can also play it during horror shows . . . you just have to change the rules a little—you kiss whenever someone gets killed. There's an entirely different feeling to it.

Is it possible to kiss over the phone?

Yes. And despite how silly it may strike you when you're making those kissey noises into the receiver, you'll actually be exciting your partner more than you could if you made the same sounds in their presence. Phone conversations, by their very nature, exclude any visual cues; they're also low in audio quality compared to in-person speech or even FM radio. As a result, the person on the other end completes the picture by filling in the missing details. According to media expert Marshall McLuhan, the net effect of this process is keen participation by the listener— the emotions get involved, and any sound that's halfway romantic will be interpreted as doubly so when transmitted via phone. The best way to kiss over the phone is to say something romantic, like, "When I see you I'm going to kiss you a hundred times," and then make the kissing sounds into the receiver. If you feel silly doing it, just remember, it won't sound silly to your listener.

What's the best way to have a kissing adventure at a party?

The greatest thing about party kisses is that you have an opportunity to kiss people who aren't your lover, and both men and women find this nerve-racking and exciting. The easiest way to do this is to organize a kissing game.

How do you play spin the bottle?

The boys and girls get in a circle. One person spins a bottle in the center of the group. Whoever it points to must kiss the spinner in front of everyone. The game is more fun if played in the dark by candlelight. When it's your turn, you may find yourself hoping that the bottle points to your favorite person. If it doesn't, you may even be tempted to cheat by stopping it somehow. Doing so is a really nice way to flirt.

What about post office?

All the boys are out of the room. One girl is in an area called the post office. You can put a few chairs around this area to give some degree of privacy. One of the other girls tells one of the guys he has some mail. He goes into the post office and is kissed. He exits and the game continues with boys being called in one by one.

What is kissing rugby?

It's a game played by college students. Guys and gals sit in a circle, and each guy gets a number, each gal a letter. The guy who is *it* goes into the middle of the circle and calls someone of the same sex out to protect him. This second guy also comes out into the circle. (Note that the person who is *it* doesn't really know who he is calling out, since it is done by letter/number.) Then the person who is *it* calls out someone from the opposite sex. This person is the attacker. (Again, the person doesn't know who he's getting!)

And now the fun begins . . .

The attacker must catch the person who is *it* and kiss him before the attacker gets caught and kissed by the protector. If the person who is *it* gets caught, he stays *it*. If the attacker gets caught, she becomes *it*. It's really nowhere near as rough as it sounds, because there are some important rules: No getting on your feet: you may only walk on your knees. No leaving the circle. No kissing anywhere but the face, and no kissing on the lips.

Kissing rugby works best with people you don't know well, and it gets better after a few rounds, because, for example, if you're a guy and you like the gal who is letter *E,* you know which letter to call the next time you're *it* . . .

What is a group kiss?

A group kiss occurs when three or more people kiss simultaneously. It's always an amazing experience for all involved. For example, at a party, two girls will kiss one guy, both kissing him on the lips at the same time. (For some reason, I've never had a guy object to this.) Or one girl will be kissed by two guys. At our kissing shows, the group kiss fascinates college audiences who love to see people being kissed by others they're not going out with. Three-way kisses always provoke riotous laughter and excitement in both demonstrators and audience. In real life, group kisses can be organized most easily at the conclusion of parties, when people are often in a lighthearted mood.

I want to kiss my date for the first time. How can I get her in the mood?

The mood has to be something you both feel. There are no magic words you can say, but the best thing to do is deepen your romantic encounter. The ways to do this involve conversation, being together for an extended time, being physically close together, sitting side by side, walking together, and working on fun tasks together. Maintain eye contact until you start to feel like you're falling into her eyes. Let the situation warm up so that you feel a magnetic attraction toward her that you can't resist. If you feel it and she feels it, then you can't go wrong.

If you had only one chance to kiss a woman and the possibility of that relationship having any future at all depended on that kiss, how would you kiss her?

A true friendship or relationship is much stronger than one kiss. But whatever happens, for a first kiss you should give her a gentle lip kiss to test the waters. See how she responds; if she doesn't seem to like it, back off. If she smiles and seems pleased, just take it where it leads. But don't french-kiss her on the first date unless she gives you some tongue first. If you really want to impress her . . . then reread the previous sentence, underline it, memorize it, and write it on a little slip of paper that you can take with you on your first date with her.

Is there any way to figure out how a girl likes to be kissed without asking her?

You can usually tell how a girl likes to be kissed by how she kisses you. So notice how she kisses you, then kiss her back the same way. But also try to add a few things of your own now and then. Also remember that most girls don't like tongue kisses too soon or all the time.

How can a boy signal a girl that he wants to kiss?

Let her see the backs of your hands, which many women find a turn-on. Get close to her physically. Look into her eyes without blinking for prolonged periods of time in a romantic way. (Romantic means without staring her down. If you do this wrong, e.g., if you just bore your eyes into her, she'll think you're on amphetamines.) Most important, talk to her about her day, ask her how she feels about things, listen carefully to what she says, and carry on a real conversation with her. When you're close enough to touch her, find an excuse to straighten some article of her clothing, brush a piece of lint off her arm, or touch her hair. If she flinches, turns pale, or jumps back, you've made your move too soon. But if all goes right, you'll feel an electric current making you tingle and a magnetic attraction drawing you closer together. If she doesn't get the message, you might as well break down and say something, such as, "I've been trying to signal my interest in kissing you all night, but you're acting like I'm from the IRS."

How can a girl signal a boy that she wants a kiss?

You signal a boy that you want to kiss him by standing in front of him, giving him a dreamy smile, making plenty of eye contact, wetting your lips, making your lower lip hang open just a little bit, and looking cute and flirty. When you talk to him don't answer quickly . . . allow a big pause before you say anything . . . and during that pause, lean forward with your mouth slightly open, as if dying of thirst! Then utter a few halting syllables. Do this enough, and most guys will get the hint. If you want to perfect your technique, watch the television show *Gilligan's Island* and imitate the way Ginger acts, or study the way Marilyn Monroe talks to men in her movies. But be prepared to have men suddenly flocking your way!

How can I make a lip kiss extra special?

The answer is by doing a variety of things with your lips, tongue, breath, and nose during the kiss. Rock your head back and forth until you feel like you're getting dizzy. Try little pecks on the lips. You can inhale gently, breathing in your lover's delicious fragrance. Suck one of his lips, then the other. Gently nibble on the lip. Tentatively, lick his lips, as if you're testing to see if he's salty enough to eat. Squeeze his lips between your own. Try different pressure—sometimes pushing gently, sometimes hard against his lips. Act like his lips are a dish on which remain a few morsels of your favorite food, and with a kind of vacuuming action, try to suck up all the crumbs. In this way, you'll add so much variety to your basic kisses, you'll easily be able to waste entire afternoons doing nothing more than lip smooching.

How can I prevent my lips from drying out?

Lip balm or Chap Stick. If you use it regularly, your lips will not dry out. Some kissers take breaks to apply it, just like taking a pit stop.

What foods or drinks make kissing more tasty?

Some people find that beer can be a nice flavor in a lover's mouth. Lots of people like minty tastes. Cinnamon is also a favorite. Most candies with a flavor are ideal for giving your mouth a nice kissing taste.

When should I kiss on a date?

The easiest time is when you're about to say good night. That's usually easy because it's expected. Some people, however, complain that dates try to get good-night kisses even if there was no romantic connection during the evening. So if you're thinking of kissing good-bye, ask yourself whether you felt pins and needles or some other romantic excitement during the date. If not, you might want to refrain from trying a good-night kiss.

If you do kiss good night, you may find that first kiss leading to more kisses. Which is one reason to end dates early—so that the kissing can begin! Another popular time to kiss is when meeting your date at the beginning of the evening. These hello kisses can set a pleasant romantic tone for the rest of the night.

What's your final bit of advice?

Highly recommended is this little trick: Kiss your lover good-bye *twice* as much as you usually do! Stretch it out. Think of Shakespeare's "parting is such sweet sorrow" scene in *Romeo and Juliet* for inspiration on how to milk a leave-taking for all it's worth.

Then kiss, and kiss again!

A kiss good-bye is like a promise.

And if you kiss good-bye, you'll remain in your lover's heart until you meet again.

$\mathcal{I}$ NDEX

Numbers in **bold** type indicate primary references.

$8.95/$13.99 Can.

The world-famous kissing coach answers all your burning
questions on the romantic art of kissing

Now that his first book, *The Art of Kissing,* is an international
best-seller, kissing expert William Cane receives thousands of questions every year on the subject of how to kiss—everything from
"What's the best way to kiss someone for the first time?" to "How do
I know if I'm doing it right?" to "What if my tongue is too short?"
The result, eagerly awaited by kissing connoisseurs around the
world, is *The Art of Kissing Book of Questions and Answers.*

Here, everyone who loves to pucker up will find expert advice on:
• Improving your technique • Mastering the French kiss, the neck
kiss, and other favorites • Perfecting the most unusual, exciting,
and romantic [...] what your kissing partner really
wants—and exc[...]sies • Overcoming shyness
and fear of in[...]ant first kiss • Trying out
popular kisses from around the world, including ten new kisses
• and more.

**Lovers everywhere will savor this playful, passionate guide to life's
sweetest pleasure. So pucker up!**

William Cane is the pen name for Michael Christian,
the best-selling author of *The Art of Kissing, The Art of
Hugging,* and *The Book of Kisses.* He lectures on kissing
around the country and lives in Brookline, Massachusetts.

Cover design by Mary Ann Smith
Cover photo by Jon Feingersh / The Stock Market
Author photo by Terri McCarthy

St. Martin's Griffin
175 Fifth Avenue, New York, N.Y. 10010
Distributed by McClelland & Stewart Inc. in Canada
PRINTED IN THE UNITED STATES OF AMERICA

ISBN 0-312-19830-2

50895>

9 780312 198305